Shamanism

Shamanism is one of the earliest and farthest-reaching magical and religious traditions, vestiges of which still underlie the major religious faiths of the modern world. The function of the shaman is to show his or her people the unseen powers behind the mere appearances of nature, as experienced through intuition, in trance states or during ecstatic mystical visions. Shamans possess healing powers, communicate with the dead and the world beyond and influence the weather and movements of hunting animals. The psychological exaltation of shamanic trance states is similar to the ecstasies of Yogis, Christian mystics and Dervishes.

Shamanism: A Concise Introduction traces the development of shamanism in its many fascinating global manifestations. Looking at shamanic practices from Siberia to China and beyond, it provides an accessible guide to one of the world's most ancient, notorious and frequently misrepresented spiritual traditions. Placing special emphasis on the climatic, geographic and cultural pressures under which shamanic customs arose and continue to be observed, Margaret Stutley summarizes and clearly explains the logic of a faith whose fantastical elements hold a special place in popular imagination.

Margaret Stutley is a leading scholar of world religions and folk tradition, and is the author of several books including *Hinduism* (1989), *Ancient Indian Magic and Folklore* (1980) and *An Introduction to Magical Elements in the Bible* (1991).

Shamanism
An Introduction

Margaret Stutley

Routledge
Taylor & Francis Group

LONDON AND NEW YORK

To Enys Davies, Christopher Aslet and
Emyr Owen Jones for all their
encouragement and help.

First published 2003 by Routledge
11 New Fetter Lane, London EC4P 4EE

Simultaneously published in the USA and Canada
by Routledge
29 West 35th Street, New York, NY 10001

Routledge is an imprint of the Taylor & Francis Group

© 2003 Margaret Stutley

Typeset in Palatino by
Keystroke, Jacaranda Lodge, Wolverhampton
Printed and bound in Great Britain by TJ International Ltd,
Padstow, Cornwall

British Library Cataloguing in Publication Data
A catalogue record for this book is available from the British
Library

Library of Congress Cataloging in Publication Data
A catalog record for this book has been requested

ISBN 0–415–27317–X (hbk)
ISBN 0–415–27318–8 (pbk)

Contents

Acknowledgements

I should like to take this opportunity to thank the experts in the field of shamanic studies for my extensive use of the following books:

U. Harva, *Shamanic Costume and its Significance*, Annales universitatis fennicae aboensis (Turku) series B, 1 (2), 1922; M. Hoppál (ed.), *Shamanism in Eurasia*, Göttingen, 1984, 'Shamanism: An Archaic and/or Recent System of Beliefs', in *Ural-Altic Yearbook*, 57, pp. 121–140, 1985, with V. Diószegi, *Shamanism in Siberia*, Akadémiai Kiadó, Budapest, 1978, and with A-L. Siikala, *The Rite Technique of the Siberian Shaman*, F.F. Communications 220, Helsinki, 1978.

Margaret Stutley

Introduction

Many shamanic belief systems are of a great age and have gained in complexity over the centuries. They are found throughout the vast regions of Central Asia and Siberia, and to a lesser extent in Europe and other countries especially North and South America, but this work deals primarily with Eurasian shamanism. Many beliefs appear to have originated among the Palaeolithic nomad hunter-gatherers.

It is difficult to comprehend the size of Eurasia. Siberia alone is as big as the United States of America and Europe put together. Consequently, it has enormous geographical, ecological, linguistic, ethnic and cultural diversity. It contains also the world's largest, oldest and deepest freshwater lake – Baikal – in which live a large number of flora and fauna known only in this area. It includes the only freshwater seal, the nerpa (*Phoca siberica*). But now this most valuable ecosystem is in need of protection from the effluent of towns, factories, logging, mining, agriculture, acid rain and ranching.

To the west, east and south the country is bounded by high mountains, while the north is open to fearsome Arctic storms. The only way into the country is through a break in the Ural mountains, the route taken in the late sixteenth century by Tsarist forces who gradually gained control of the whole region. Much of the north consists of tundra, snow-covered for eight or nine months of the year, but during the short summer masses of flowers and vegetation appear, although the earth remains eternally frozen a foot or two down. Further south is the taiga, the world's largest forest of conifers and birches covering two-thirds of the land. The climate is harsh with extremes of temperature and long winters when the temperature drops to minus 65°C with an icy wind chill, which explains why this immensely rich land of mineral deposits and timber is so thinly populated.

The indigenous Siberians live in extended family groups, sometimes far apart, but having some connection with other clans or tribes. As the climate is unsuitable for agriculture, most of the inhabitants are herders or owners of reindeer, cattle or horses, living a precarious nomadic or semi-nomadic existence.

Although shamanism had flourished for centuries, its slow decline occurred when the Tsarist troops entered the country. Nevertheless it took nearly 400 years before many of its traditions were destroyed or driven underground during Stalin's ferocious purges in the 1930s. Many shamans were executed; others sent to labour camps. Today, there are vastly more Russians in Siberia than Siberians, so now making it impossible for them to regain control of their own land. There are only about one and a half million native Siberians divided into a number of tribes, the largest and most successful being the Buriats and Yakuts.

Shamanism should not be thought of as a single centrally organized religion, as there are many variations. Yet despite these cultural differences three things are shared by all forms of shamanism: (1) belief in the existence of a world of spirits, mostly in animal form that are capable of acting on human beings. The shaman is required to control or cooperate with these good and bad spirits for the benefit of his community. (2) The inducing of trance by ecstatic singing, dancing and drumming, when the shaman's spirit leaves his or her body and enters the supernatural world. (3) The shaman treats some diseases, usually those of a psychosomatic nature, as well as helping the clan members to overcome their various difficulties and problems.

Some ethnographers have suggested that shamanism should not be studied only for its religio-magical viewpoints, but more importantly for the philosophical, naturalist and medical elements, especially the psychiatric methods that appear to be the most effective, although they pre-date by many centuries the discoveries of Western psychiatry.

Krader (1956, pp. 282–292) has pointed out that shamanism can be used in various ways since it is an element in *all* religions, such as in the ecstatic, charismatic leaders of Buddhist, Jewish, Christian, Islamic and other cults and sects; or as a religion associated with specific cult practices – the World Tree, the Fire-cult, Soul-loss, Soul-flight and so on. Similarly, Voight (1977) claims that the origins of most religions can be explained completely by shamanistic analogies.

Spirit possession is central to all forms of shamanism, and also has a central position in religious phenomenology and psychology. Lewis (1994, p. 24) has pointed out that it is at the root of mysticism, including the concept of the Holy Ghost, Dervish dancing, fire-walking, transvestism, aggressive messianic cults, and all major religions based on the notion of a supreme spiritual deity.

The name 'shamanism' was invented by Europeans, so giving the impression that there was only one fixed belief system, instead of a number of disparate beliefs having many facets and continually increasing as new situations arise, although retaining many of the old beliefs and overlapping traditions. In the same way, Europeans lumped together the vast uncoordinated, amorphous mass of new and old religious cults, customs and practices of India and called them Hinduism; its adherents know it as the Eternal Law (*sanatana dharma*).

The origin of the term shaman (the ecstatic one) is still disputed. The views put forward include the following: it is derived from the Tungus word *śaman*, or from the Pali term *samaṇa* (Sanskrit *śramaṇa*) and the Chinese *sha-men*. This derivation is often given in modern books on the subject, although it was disproved by Laufer in 1917. Others derive it from the Vedic term *śram* meaning 'to heat oneself'. This is equivalent to the Hindu term *tapas* implying 'heat' and 'potential power', a necessary part of asceticism. But Laufer and some other experts consider that shaman is a Tungus term belonging to the genuine Turko-Mongolian language, without having any connection with Indian or Chinese terms. However, the great Russian scholar Shirokogoroff (1923) does not agree, and claims that the term *śaman* is foreign to the Tungusic tongue.

Other tribes have different terms for shaman but as the religion was first recorded by Europeans among the Tungus their term is used. The Turkic-speaking peoples use the term *kam*; the Yakuts call it *oyuna*; the Samoyeds, *tadibey*; the Yukaghirs, *alma*; the Buriats, *buge*, and so on.

In spite of the vast literature that has accumulated on the subject during the past 200 years many early shamanic beliefs and much symbolism still remain unknown. Some experts are not even convinced that it constitutes a religion, although much of it is concerned with the supernatural world of spirits, deities, demons, ecstasy and magic, all of which are found in the major and minor religious systems of the world.

V. M. Mikhailovski, at the end of the nineteenth century, considered that shamanism represented a universal form of religion. At the beginning of the twentieth century, the Swedish scholar J. Stadling regarded it as an animistic concept of the world and hence representing an early part of religious thinking. Some modern writers share the same view, although animism also exists in areas where shamanism is unknown. Although animistic beliefs are regarded as inferior, the manifestation of the sacred in a specific mountain, animal, tree or stone is no less mysterious than its manifestation in a deity. To Bogoras (1904) and Vdovin (1973) shamanism represented a certain stage in the development of religion. To Hans Findeisen and Vilmo Diószegi it is a form of religion, while to A-L. Siikala (with M. Hoppál, 1992, p. 19) it is a phenomenon in the realm of magic and religion. But some writers regard shamans and their practices as aberrations or frauds, as psychopaths or as related to hysteria, neurosis and epilepsy. Yet the majority agree that it does contain certain magico-religious elements. However, recent research indicates that shamanism represents the earliest basic religious experiences of mankind and therefore is important for the understanding of all human culture, including Stone Age beliefs, and for the symbolism of the ancient rock paintings of Eurasia, dating from about 3000 BCE to about 100 BCE. Mircea Eliade and some other writers see an early form of shamanism in the Lascaux cave paintings, especially in the depiction of a bird, a tutelary spirit, perched on a pole.

The rock paintings of Lascaux and those of Siberia were part of the magico-religious activities that took place on the sites, being an important aspect of the social life of the people. The figures depict ancestors, spirits, heroes, shamans and animals.

According to Whitney's *Century Dictionary*, the earliest religions of Sumeria and Akkad contained some shamanistic elements, which appear also in the epic poetry of the Odyssey, and in the Finnish Kalevala. E. Rohde (1893) saw shamanic influences in ancient Greek religion, especially in the ecstatic Bacchanalianism of Thrace.

According to Wilhelm Schmidt the religion of the Inner Asian nomads was shamanic and associated with southern matriarchal communities. Some writers agree with the above view, since women initially performed important functions that were later taken over by men. This may explain the transvestism practised today by some Eurasian shamans.

There have never been any entirely 'new' religions in spite of what their respective adherents believe, because the message is always reinterpreted or completely recast as well as being influenced by neighbouring beliefs. In the case of shamanism they included the animistic, pre-Buddhist Bon religion of Tibet, and later Tibetan, Indian and Chinese Buddhism, Hinduism, Taoism and Zoroastrianism.

Various mind-altering drugs are used by some Eurasian shamans during their ecstatic performances, but not always, since many shamans rely solely on their own powers to reach the supernatural world of spirits. The most usual hallucinogenic is the *fly agaric* mushroom which grows over much of northern Siberia and in many other countries including the United Kingdom. The sacred and recreational drink of the Buriats is *tarasun*, a mixture of wine and milk; the Yakuts use *koumiss*, fermented mare's milk.

At the beginning of the twentieth century an amalgamation of Dzhungar Buddhism and shamanic ideas occurred called Burkhanism – a Mongolian name for a manifestation of the Buddha. It is also known as the 'White faith' (*ak di'an*). It strongly rejects Russian Orthodox Christianity.

Now, after 200 years of persecution by Tsarist officials, Orthodox Christianity and Communism, shamanism has come out into the open, and there is a considerable amount of interest in it from students of comparative religion and folklorists.

1

Male and Female Shamans

Shamans have long been associated with hunter-gatherers and members of nomadic societies. Shamans advise the community when hunting is unsuccessful, or whenever crises occur in the harsh climate of extreme cold and the ever-present risk of starvation and disease. These societies are the nearest one can get to a 'classless', loosely stratified society.

The shaman, in common with the priest of other religions, does not bring about any social reform for he is conservative and supports the established order. For thousands of years the shaman has protected mankind's mythological knowledge. Thus he is a completely integrated part of the culture, whereas the prophet is a reformer-innovator.

The main purposes of male and female shamans are connected with divination, understanding Nature, healing the sick and, especially, preserving the psychomental equilibrium of the clan, so preventing the spread of psychic epidemics and psychosomatic illnesses. He is helped by his spirits who give him knowledge far in excess of that available to ordinary mortals. Shamans have peculiar brilliant eyes which enable them to see spirits as well as being sensitive to any change in the nearby psychic atmosphere. They uphold clan values, and bring about harmony between human beings and supernatural forces.

Some individuals may receive their calling any time between the ages of 6 and 50 but the majority are about 20 years old. Some Uzbek shamanesses received the call after marriage and after having had up to three children.

Both male and female Khanty shamans are worshipped as ancestral shamans in sacred groves where images of the ancestors are kept.

The making of a shaman

Although there are many different beliefs concerning the making of a shaman, it is usual for him or her to have a twin spirit in the shape of an animal which becomes the chief spirit or *alter ego*. After the novice is fully trained, the spirit returns to the middle earth where it settles on a larch tree. Henceforth, it becomes the main assistant during ritual performances. Another method is to possess an ancestral spirit which may be a generalized spirit of a certain line, or the soul of a particular shaman ancestor, or both at the same time. Shirokogoroff points out that shamans and initiates 'practice the conscious loss of consciousness'.[1]

Part of the training includes aggravating the nervous system by undergoing specific austerities, experiencing and controlling trances during which the spirit world is visited and mastering the neuro-physiological processes of one's own body. A-L. Siikala has pointed out that a person with normal nerves may achieve a state of trance, but people of greater sensitivity do find it easier.[2] The so called 'shamanic-illness' which may occur at this time appears to be the result of auto-suggestion and what is expected of shamans. It seems also that shamanizing usually effects a cure.

The initiate often retired to a quiet place seeking spiritual experiences, composing his or her own songs supposedly with the help of the spirits and learning the topography of the other world. During this time the spirit of an ancestor shaman appears. The initiate may feel that the spirits are destroying the old ego and body by dissecting it, after which he or she becomes a shaman, able to see things and worlds that are hidden from the uninitiated. The importance of dismemberment and the initiate's rebirth is found also in animal ceremonialism where the bones are the points of attachment for the soul. After initiation the shaman demonstrates various powers in public rites for the benefit of the community. He or she is now a psychotherapeutic healer, having undergone both mental and physical suffering and a long training that enables him or her to train others. The shaman is also a mediator between the supra-normal and normal worlds and so restores a proper balance. It is important to remember that shamans' experiences are based on the beliefs of each individual's own culture, and what has been learned in altered states of consciousness; thus a shaman meets his spirit-helper, whereas a Christian mystic may see Jesus or the Virgin Mary.

The Chukchis believe that everything lives and therefore even apparently inanimate objects possess some kind of soul principle. For this reason the shaman's spirits may even include stones or household utensils.

The *ajami* spirit of the Nanai people is inherited and becomes the tutelary spirit of the initiatory period as well as providing the spirits necessary for shamanizing. This spirit wife or husband has an erotic relationship with the shaman. Similarly the transvestite shamans among the Siberian and inner Asian tribal peoples often have a spirit lover.

When the performance is dealing mainly with soul flight or with the shaman's journey to the lower world the emphasis is not so much on talking to the spirits. The trance state usually ends in loss of consciousness. Later the spirits may be called back by singing and drumming and may answer questions from the assembly.

A shaman may feel his or her vocation spontaneously, or through a long-term, painful illness, or through a vivid dream or vision or by means of meditation. It may be assisted by fasting, isolation, exhaustion, repetitive music, or by narcotics, tobacco, alcohol and so on. But merely consuming drugs without the necessary mental training, even if carried on for many years, will not lead to spirituality – a fact seen clearly in the drug culture of the Western world.

Some ethnographers consider that women were the first shamans, and that they appeared in the matriarchal period when women were far greater magicians than their male counterparts and also performed important clan functions later taken over by male shamans. This may explain the fact that a number of male shamans practise transvestism, thereby indicating the former importance of shamanesses. When a Yakut shaman approaches the Master of the Forest, he dons a woman's headdress and carries a bow. Siikala points out that transvestism when shamanizing 'is a typical feature, also in Palaeo-Asian shamanism'.[3]

Another view is that a woman was the first human being to receive shamanic powers which she transmitted later to her son who became the first male shaman. Usually the wives of clan-founders are mentioned together with their husbands in clan incantations, although a number of women are invoked alone as ancestors. Often they are unmarried mothers whose sons' births were of a miraculous nature.[4]

Some ethnographers regard shamans as unbalanced, neurotic individuals. This seems unlikely as neurotics are entirely wrapped up in themselves and have no desire to help others. In fact shamans may be innately creative, balanced and with more mental capacity than their people. They understand much of the phenomena of nature, and are ready to help their community. More especially they function as intermediaries between the people and the spirits of other worlds.

Although ventriloquism was employed to give the impression that spirits were speaking from different parts of the dwelling, shamanism consists of much more than mere conjuring tricks, for the practitioners themselves are often in deep trance states, the details of which they are unable to recall.

There is a hereditary rite to claim a shaman's function, which may be transmitted in a family equally to boys or girls. When not represented on Earth by a shaman or shamaness it becomes dangerous to its owner; therefore such a lineage tries to avoid not having a living shamanic representative.

The Chukchi shamaness S. Telpina related that she had suffered severe mental illness for three years during which time her family ensured that she did not injure herself. Yet when finally she accepted the call to become a shamaness her recovery began. Accepting the call involves accepting several spirits as protectors or helpers, thereby opening the way to communication with the whole spirit world. Sometimes the call involves hearing an 'inner voice' (also experienced by some Christians) or it may be triggered by some animal, plant, or other natural object which appears at the right time, but if the slightest lack of harmony occurs between the shaman and the spirits, he or she dies immediately. Paradoxically, it is also believed by Chukchis that a woman is by nature a shaman and therefore does not need any preparation for her calling. However, today it depends on personal ability irrespective of gender, although the majority of shamans among the Manchus have always been women.

A Nivkhi shamaness claimed that she could heal people but only when in an ecstatic state and with the help of living animals and birds. During the performance she held a black, undoctored dog on a leash which is called the 'song-leash' without which she could not see the spirits. Only the dog knew where to find the animals (embodying the spirits) that she needed to communicate with.[5]

Today shamanesses are requested to perform divination mostly in connection with healing, preventing deceit and fraud and finding lost animals and objects; occasionally they may be asked to divine for clan affairs. But the women are prohibited from ascending sacred mountains, entering a forge or stepping over hunting implements or over a male shaman's paraphernalia, because menstruation would adversely affect his utensils. It was also believed that menstrual blood prevents a person who is in a transformed state from recovering his or her normal state. (It is interesting that the Church of England and Wales required women to be 'churched' after giving birth. This archaic rite lasted until about the middle of the twentieth century.) Shamanesses were also prohibited from attending bloody sacrifices held in the open air. Nevertheless, two famous mythical shamanesses, Asujkhan and Khusujkhen, sacrificed a mare, a ram and a goat in order to obtain the boy Bulagat, one of the main ancestors of the Buriats.

Transvestism

In 1968, Basilov visited the village of Cavo to meet an old Uzbek transvestite shaman called Tašmat-bola (born 1886), the only son of a rich man. In his youth he was a good drummer, dancer and singer and he became a shaman and was blessed by a shamaness. He acquired a number of helping spirits (*paris*) who enabled him to heal people by divining which consisted of throwing a piece of cotton wool into water and watching its movements, thereby providing the required information as to the cause of the diseases and the cure. It was said that if he refused to wear women's clothes as demanded by his spirits, they would suffocate him in the night. Perhaps this indicated that his own spirits were female.

When engaged in healing serious diseases Tašmat shamanized by calling his spirits, beating his drum and crying out the names of the spirits. When they appeared he exorcized the hostile spirits causing illness, and still drumming he constantly repeated these words: 'Go away, go away!' Aided by his helping spirits he 'tied' the hostile ones saying: 'A horned snake comes, tie! A lame *pari* comes, tie!' and so on.

Then a woman near the patient ties a knot on a specially prepared thread thereby 'locking in' the spirit and draining its strength. Sometimes a hen was killed and its blood smeared on to the patient and the bleeding hen pressed against the heart while the body remained warm, after which it was given to a dog, probably in the hope that the disease would be transferred to the animal. This was a common practice in several cultures including the ancient Vedic religion of India.

Before shamanizing Tašmat lighted a lamp and placed in it a sorghum stalk soaked in grease at one end and with red, white and black shredded rags attached to the other end. This lamp was set up for the spirits.

Tašmat was said to cure people of the Evil Eye by stroking the afflicted person with bread, or with a bowl of ashes wrapped in a cloth.

Basilov points out that Tašmat combines in himself both witch-doctor and singer, a characteristic of ancient stages in the evolution of shamanism. He adds that partial feminization indicates the shamanic transvestism known among many peoples of North-east Asia and America. Transvestism is not only peculiar to shamanism but is 'related to priesthood in its most diverse forms . . . [it] was generated by the process of transition from matriarchy to patriarchy, when priestly functions became accessible to men.[6]

Transvestism also occurs when the creator is regarded as bisexual – a notion that may lead to bisexuality being seen as a spiritually superior condition to ordinary individuals. It occurs among the Kamchadals, the Asian Inuits, and, in the past, among the Koryaks, as well as in Indonesia (Sea Dyaks) and some of the Amerindians – the Arapaho, Cheyenne, Ute and others; and in South America among the Araucanians and Patagonians.[7]

Herodotus (I. 105) referred to Scythians who had a class of diviners known as *enaries* 'womanish men', who divined by willow rods, a gift from Aphrodite who sent down to them a 'women's disease'. (Tašmat's drum was sometimes replaced by a panicle of willow twigs). Hippocrates noted that the men spoke like women and did female chores. He considered that this defect was caused by horse riding. Similarly, through riding exercises the Pueblo Indians of the USA managed to cause the total loss of the male functions of those who had to change sex (such persons being needed for 'religious orgies').[8]

Androgynous male and female shamans

Some young shamans dreaded the thought of androgyny to such an extent that a number preferred suicide than meet this requirement, in spite of the fact that such individuals were highly regarded and believed to be the most powerful of all practitioners.[9]

Siikala (in *Studies on Shamanism*, pp. 56ff.) states that a typical feature of Palaeo-Asian shamanism is when a Scandinavian transvestite shaman, when shamanizing, approaches the Mistress of the Forest.

Some Chukchi clans had androgynous male and female shamans who had ritually and psychologically 'changed sex'. With the aid of spirits they become attractive to the opposite sex from whom they choose their lovers, husbands or wives. Transvestite men adopt women's clothes and ways; the females are then 'transformed' into men, wear male attire, speak like men and learn to use weapons. They find girls who are ready to become their 'wives'. In this case, a gastrocnemius obtained from the leg of a reindeer sometimes serves as a male organ. If children are desired a marriage will be arranged with suitable young neighbours.[10]

The androgynous state transcends the pairs of opposites and embraces all contraries, thus retaining perfect harmony and equilibrium. Therefore the male or female shaman is a 'healed healer' who, by means of a personal rite of transformation, integrates many aspects of the life experience, including body and spirit, maleness and femaleness, good and bad, the individual and the community and the past, present and future. Finally, totality is attained that previously existed when the many were the One.

Those cultures that have a male female polarity theme of an androgynous supreme being believe such a being to possess enormous universal power from which all the pairs of opposites have sprung. Such beings include the androgynous form of the ancient Egyptian god of the Nile, Hapi and Nu, god of the primeval waters from which the world was created; the male female form of Śiva Ardhanārī; the Tantric supreme being includes both male and female elements; in northern Australia the mighty god Ungud is the bisexual creator; and in the Bible (Genesis I. 27) it is written that 'God created man in his own image . . . male and female'.

Most shamans were male in the eighteenth and nineteenth centuries, yet even in many of these patriarchal societies there was always an important minority of shamanesses, and all Siberian tribes believed in a benign, much-loved, female divinity. Mythologically, great power was attributed to women. From the above it appears that in aboriginal Siberia the position of women was much superior to what it became later. (This also occurred in Vedism, early Hinduism, in Buddhism and also in Christianity.) By the time shamanism had declined in the nineteenth century, shamanesses became more common, using their skills mainly in folk medicine, and solving the everyday problems of the clans. The Tadzhik shamaness Ouliia-folbin has great presence, is resolute and self-confident. When calling the spirits she sits on a prayer rug beating her drum. Her spirits sit on a white cloth on the wall.

Before the sixteenth century, shamanism was the main religion of Mongolia. Shamans and witches favoured owls, although the birds were feared by the people. Owl feathers decorate many shamanic costumes, especially on headgear.[11]

Among the Tungus-speaking peoples there are male and female professional shamans, as well as minor ones who perform elementary acts including interpreting dreams, divining, finding lost animals and practising folk medicine. Traditionally the Tungus believe that a special tree stands between day and night. On it are nine nests placed on top of each other. In these nests the souls of shamans are hatched.

Birds have long been associated with shamanic rites. Often the shaman imagines himself to be a bird flying up to the heavens, or descending to the underworld. For this reason the breast-cover of the ritual costume is in the shape of a bird's breastbone. It is interesting to note that the same Chinese character denotes both 'shaman' and 'bird'.

The Tungus perform an autumnal sacrifice (corresponding roughly to November to January) during which the shaman drums as a pig is sacrificed. The animal's heart is removed and the blood made into sausages. The meat and bones are boiled, then put together as if the animal were alive and placed on the offering table for the spirits. Only by 'steam' (aroma) can the spirits savour the offering. Similarly, the Hebrew Yahweh loved the smell of burnt offerings that wafted up to him. Formerly, stone cup-like bowls were used. Some of them have been excavated on the banks of the Amur river, and are still known in

North-eastern Asia and America. They are part of the Palaeolithic complex in Europe, and in Neolithic Japan.

Although sacrifices are most important for influencing spirits, there is no term for sacrifice in the Tungus dialects. Instead the general term 'to pray' is used or 'to feed' the spirits.

Among the Samoyeds, Buriats and Ostyaks the shaman's office is hereditary. A Buriat child who is a potential shaman may experience visions, loves solitude, is often absorbed in deep meditation, has strange dreams and sometimes has fits culminating in unconsciousness. No one under 20 years old can become a shaman. In other clans certain gifted individuals may show a predisposition for shamanizing. They may have hallucinations, enter easily into ecstatic trance states or may be epileptic. In the latter case, they can control their epileptic attacks which ordinary sufferers cannot.

A Buriat novice shaman is usually taught by an old shaman who tells him how to summon different kinds of spirits and how to deal with them. As a preparatory 'gathering of shamanistic powers' the novice often spends long periods of solitude in forests or remains in the house.

According to the Altaians no one becomes a shaman of his own free will, but it comes upon him like a hereditary disease. It is the ancestor's spirit that 'leaps' upon him. When a spirit enters a shamaness her stomach swells up as if pregnant. When it leaves, her stomach returns to its normal state.[12]

The novice Koryak shaman needs to contact spirits that will protect him. These spirits sometimes appear as birds or animals – a wolf, raven, seagull, bear or plover – or in the form of men when he is in the desert. They command him to accept his calling or to die; apparently there is no alternative. The novice then has to learn singing, dancing, various conjuring tricks, ventriloquism, and how to beat the drum. Occasionally Nivkhi shamans may die at the end of their songs when the spirit 'which inspires them leaves the tip of the singer's tongue'.[13] Many of the songs are repetitive and when accompanied by drumming enable the shaman's mind to enter an altered state of consciousness. This resembles the repetitive words and beat of pop music today. Drum-beating requires both skill and endurance, but no signs of fatigue must be shown for the shaman is sustained entirely by the spirits. He also has to keep strictly to a special diet.

Posts linked with cords are sometimes set up by Yakut shamans to function as a map of the supernatural world along which they travel while giving a commentary of the sights seen. Musicians were often employed, including the players of Siberian guitars or mouth-harps. Each shaman has a 'beast mother' who is his soul (*kut*) or invisible double. This mother has the form of a bird with iron feathers that sits on the branches of the shaman's special tree.

Among the Nenets people, a potential shaman is determined from his or her birth by a distinctive mark being a pellicle on the crown of the head, or by a birthmark. At puberty the future shaman develops peculiar signs, being tormented by strange visions and experiencing various illnesses.

Dragonfly shamans

The *duńd* (dragonfly) shamans were the most powerful among the Kets, although seldom seen. Their first shaman was the mythical *doh*. Their mother was mistress of the warm upper world. Thunder and cranes were their brothers and swans their sisters. The work of the *duńds* was limited to the warm season starting with the birds' arrival and lasting until they flew away. The shamans wore iron headgear on which were thundercloud images and longitudinal bars with knife-like tips.

Shamans of different categories on Earth and in the upper world went different ways on the 'roads' of the air that led through the circles and planes of the upper world, but only the great road of the *duńd* was walked by the first shaman *doh*. The road ended in the seventh circle, the 'sky's end', where dwelt the supreme deity Es. To the Kets the 'roads' were entirely realistic; the *duńd* road ended in the sea covered with waterlilies, their broad leaves depicted on drums or flat pendants on which the *duńd* shamans sat.[14] The Kets of the Yenisei north have two types of shamans – those dealing with the Earth and those dealing with the lower world, who fight against hostile spirits and all things harmful to the clan. They impersonate bears or bear-like creatures, as well as retaining the memory of a special class of shamans called dragonfly (*duńd*), who were connected exclusively with the sacral world.

The highest Ket initiation was a long process. It comprised seven three-year stages. The stage the initiand had reached was indicated by the insignia on his costume. Ket women could be shamans but only of the earthly world – the upper sacral world was accessible only to men.

Some shamans are hostile and attack others, often by adversely influencing their mental states. A Birarčen shaman when fighting never lifts up his arms but keeps them close to his body to protect the holes made in the sides of his costume, through which his adversaries' spirits may enter him.[15] Such malevolent shamans were greatly feared because they catch the souls of other shamans on their way back from the lower world.

Novice Manchurian and Inuit shamans, in common with Hindu ascetics and Tibetan Tantric yogins, must prove their magical powers by resisting extreme cold: the ability to do so is indicative of having reached a superhuman state. Sometimes the ecstatic state does not occur until the shaman is 'heated'. Narcotics are sometimes used to attain magical heat and the burning of certain herbs which increases 'power'. Narcotic intoxication represents 'death'. In other words, the individual has left his body and become temporarily a ghost or spirit. A pure opiate narcotic and a derivative of the opium plant produce among other things dilation of cutaneous blood-vessels and warming of the skin. Some regular users experience near ecstatic and often intense sexual feelings.[16] Hallucinogens often give a sense of the ineffable and greater suggestibility, or a sense of depersonalization or transcendence may occur.

A great performance by a shaman was 'attended' by the koori bird, the shaman's chief helping spirit that is also associated with the World Tree without which the rite could not be performed, for the bird cannot 'exist' without the World (or shaman's) Tree.

Secret language

Efforts now are being made to reconstruct the so-called 'secret language' of the Siberian Turkic shamans, and also that used in other areas of Siberia. Vestiges of the language remain in the incomprehensible refrains repeated in some shamanic performances; but a specific secret language has been verified among the Lapps, Inuits,

Ostyaks, Chukchis, Yakuts and Tungus. The complete reconstruction has proved impossible as much shamanic lore has been lost. However, it was customary to initiate shamans into the 'secret language' of spirits, and especially of animals, the shamanic experience being closely connected with the animal world, for animals are connected with worlds unknown to human beings.The shamans' secret language is an imitation of animal cries, or the sounds of birds. To know bird language enables one to understand all Nature's secrets, and to prophesy. By eating a snake or some other magical animal, bird language can be learned, for such animals are the receptacles of the souls of the dead, or are epiphanies of the gods. During the ritual the shaman moves freely through the three cosmic zones – underworld, Earth and sky – by imitating animal sounds or by magically transforming himself into an animal. In the beginning, man was friendly to animals and knew their language so that when the shaman transmogrifies into an animal it indicates that the long-lost 'paradisal' situation has been re-established.[17]

This language somewhat resembles the glossolalia of the Christians. Odd archaic words are uttered, or words from a neighbouring language. Many shamans claim it is the language of spirits. By means of this technique the shamans are no longer responsible for what they say. It may be that this is a way of entering swiftly into one's own super-consciousness, a psychological method which could be adapted without further ado by modern psychotherapy.[18] This secret language appears to resemble slightly the secret language used by early hunters to achieve successful hunting.[19] Similarly Indian Tantrists use the secret 'twilight language' (*sandhyā-bhāṣā*); Tibetan Tantrists have a secret language called the 'tongue of the dakinī', probably as a means to conceal the teaching from non initiates.

The shaman sometimes assumes a new identity and becomes an animal spirit; the 'animal language' being a variant of the secret shamanic 'spirit' tongue. The helping animal spirit to whom the shaman addresses the sacred language, or who incarnates the animal's spirit by means of dances or masks, is a way of showing that the shaman can get beyond his limiting human condition and the animal becomes his *alter ego*. Sometimes the animal may be the spirit of an ancestor and may lead the dead soul to the next world, or be an initiatory Master, but each one connects the shaman with other spiritual worlds. Since the time of the religious beliefs of the Palaeo hunters, a mystical solidarity exists between human beings and animals; thus certain people have a special rapport with animals and can really understand them, as well as sharing in their prescience and occult powers. Whenever a shaman succeeds in sharing the animal mode of being he re-establishes the mythical time before the division between man and animal had occurred.

Visualization of one's skeleton

The contemplation of one's own skeleton is part of the initiatory practices. The body must be visualized as a skeleton until nothing remains except the bones. Each body part and bone must be named in the secret language learned from one's instructor. Thus he frees himself from his transient and ethereal body and consecrates himself to his great task through his bones that will last longer after death than any other part of the body. An Inuit achieves his goal by austerity and profound meditational practices, but Siberian shamans usually witness their own dismemberment by mythical beings which, after rejoining the bones leads to a mystical rebirth, the climax of their visionary initiation. However, if any of the shaman's bones are missing a number of their blood relations must die, according to the number of missing bones; these are sacrifices to the spirits. The role of women in connection with the shaman rising from his mystical death after dismemberment is well documented in the ancient hero tales, many of which contain shamanistic elements. The dead hero is reanimated by his horse or by a younger sister going to the upper world to call the birds. The limbs and bones are placed in the right order and stepped over three times, or jumped over on horseback.[20]

Tibetan Buddhism has accepted some of the shamanic practices of the indigenous animistic Bon religion, which also advocates meditation on one's body as a skeleton to stress the inevitable destructive effect of time on the individual, since that which is composite must disintegrate. Eliade points out that similar contemplation occurs also in Christian mysticism, thereby showing 'that the ultimates attained by the early consciousnesses of archaic man remain unalterable'.[21]

Yakut shamans

Usually the future shaman is called to his profession, or chosen either by some divine being in visions, dreams, ecstasy or during illness; or by his shamanic ancestors, although they in turn had to be chosen in the dawn of time; or by an encounter with a semi-divine being or supernatural animal.

The first shaman of the Yakuts was so powerful and arrogant that he refused to recognize the supreme being who sent down fire to burn him up. His body was composed of a mass of snakes, from which a toad emerged from the flames. From this toad came the 'demons' who gave the Yakuts their outstanding male and female shamans. In another Yakut story the hero Black Hawk relates that when his bride lay dying, he prayed for a shaman to come and cure her whereupon a warm breeze blew from the east and brought heavy rain, and thunder was heard. Then out of a cloud three shamans descended and flew over the sick woman. They shamanized for three days after which the patient recovered and the shamans returned to the celestial world. Later Black Hawk married twice and from his second wife came the ancestor of the Yakut people.[22]

During ritual performances Yakut shamans experienced a controlled neuro-psychological seizure when they believed themselves to be attacked by terrible beings. Their mental state was so intense that it sometimes caused similar attacks among the audience. When dealing with minor ailments such as a simple eye disorder, the shaman spits into the patient's eye who then starts, thus causing the evil spirit to leave. Similarly, Jesus cured the deaf and dumb man by putting his fingers in his ears and touching his tongue with spittle (Mark 7. 33f.). Spittle also cured the blind man. Magical powers were believed to be in spittle for it was a vehicle of ambivalent power. The ancient Assyrians believed in the power of the 'saliva of life' and of 'death'. Because of its immense potency the Essenes were forbidden to spit, but if they did it was always to the left, the side of the demonic powers.

Among the Siberian maritime peoples of Chukotka and Kamchatka, there was little distinction between professional shamans and other people, and both individual and family shamanism existed, but these groups did not possess the elaborate costumes of the chief shamans of other groups. Instead the maritime Chukchi and Inuit shamans' garments were simpler, and decorated only with tassels and pendants of seal pup fur; no special headdress was worn.

Shamanic performances

Although most Western writers use the term 'seance' for shamanic performances, it gives the wrong impression of a quiet spiritualistic seance, whereas much of the shamanic ritual is frenzied, with blood-stirring rhythmic drumming accompanied by the screams and yells of the shaman as the spirits enter him and the heightening excitement of the audience. These performances usually take place after dark because spirits are afraid of light; the settings vary from quite small affairs to large and complex ones according to the status of the shaman and the wealth of the group. The shaman calls his helping spirits by singing and drumming – the songs describe the spirits' journey, the shaman's own journey to the other world and its topography. Sometimes he imitates the cries of his animal and bird spirits. As the ritual progresses, the drumming, dancing and singing become louder and more frenzied, during which time the performer achieves an altered state of consciousness brought about by stimulation of the nervous system, focused concentration and by the high emotional expectations of the audience. Some tribal peoples increase the effects by eating the hallucinogenic fly agaric mushrooms, by burning herbs to produce intoxicating smoke, by smoking tobacco or by drinking vodka.

The possession trance is usual among the Yukaghir, Evenki, Yakut, Manchu and Nanais, when the chief spirit helpers enter the shaman's body and speak through him imitating the supposed movements and gestures of the individual spirits. Then the shaman's assistant takes over and talks to the spirit. When shamanizing over an ill person he takes the disease-causing demon into himself. When the performance is to find a lost soul the shaman travels to the other world with his helping spirits, and in trance describes his journey until finally losing consciousness.

Before a shamanic performance in Chukotka the fly agaric mushroom (*Amanita muscaria*) was eaten only by men. The Chukchi claim that the magic mushroom took people by the hand and led them along a crooked path to the land of the dead. No doubt hallucinations, visions, self-hypnosis and extreme excitement occurred through singing and drumming, but not all the Siberian peoples use hallucinogens.

The Central Inuit shaman is protected by bear spirits acquired during a secret ceremony. Both the bear and other spirit helpers live in various objects and are known as *tornait* (plural, *tornak* singular). For example, to find the cause of illness and other calamities, the shaman sits in a darkened room and invokes *tornait* by singing and shouting, after which he announces the required atonement. When *tornait* approach the hut, it shakes, indicating that the shaman has flown away with the spirits. Ventriloquism seems to be part of these performances. Sometimes the goddess Sedna appears while the shaman is praying, whereupon ecstasy takes over and he utters a secret language. A Dravidian Vedda shaman calls the spirits (*yaku*) to accept the people's offerings; when in trance the spirits speak through him. Onlookers attending the performance may also become possessed. Most shamans experience vertigo and nausea at the beginning and end of religious performances.

Shamans are able to communicate telepathically with specific persons by thinking deeply about them. The latter may reply through a spirit-bird or animal which speaks with the person's voice.[23] Shamans often call to each other on calm nights and some Russian ethnographers have observed cases of telepathic thought transference.

The main patron or spirit of a Yakut is usually an ancestor. The patrons of great shamans may appear as an ox, stallion, elk, black bear or wolf; weaker shamans have spirits in dog or cuckoo form. During shamanizing the drum becomes 'animated' and turns into a 'horse' which carries the shaman to the realm of the spirits.[24]

The most important Altaian helping spirit is *djajuk* who lives in the sky and was sent down to Earth by Ülgen, the supreme deity of the upper world and giver of life, to fight hostile spirits in the lower world when the help of pure spirits is required who, although invisible, protect and envelop the shaman's head, shoulders and body.

Hungarian shamans

Some ethnographers consider that Hungarian shamans (*taltos*) derive from Siberian shamanism. Women and men who take up shamanism are regarded as having superhuman capacities if they are born without teeth.

The horse spirit is always a helper. Rural shamans can control the weather and avert hailstorms. Male shamans are good magicians, while shamanesses are healers, seers or necromancers. It is interesting that Diószegi, one of the leading lights on shamanism, considers that necromancy (also practised by some early Hebrews) was of shamanic origin. Formerly, shamanesses were common, as attested by a number of 'single female graves of the pagan period . . . found in present day Hungary with rich grave furniture'.[25]

Chinese shamanesses

It is known that there were large numbers of shamanesses in China during the second century. The fourth-century work Chin Shu (*History of the Chin Dynasty*) relates that at one time shamanesses performed the family ancestral sacrifices. In about 460 a Liu Sung emperor engaged them to invoke the spirit of his dead consort. Similar necro-mantic rites had been performed for the emperor Han Wu Ti of the second century BCE. A ninth-century story shows that these women used ventriloquism and were expert exorcists, but later, during the Sung dynasty, they were fiercely persecuted, whereupon many of the shamanic elements in Taoism were driven underground to become yet another secret society among many that flourished in Chinese society. Over the centuries shamanism gradually fused with the pseudo-sciences of divination, astrology, geomancy, oneiromancy, written charms and the use of talismans.

According to the second-century Chinese dictionary, *Shuo-wen*, compiled by Xu Shen, 'the character *wu* [meaning shamaness] is a pictograph representing a woman who serves the "formless" and can by dancing cause the deities to descend'.[26] *Wu* means both 'shamaness' and 'to dance'; male shamans are known as *hsi*. Chinese historical documents attest that Mongolian shamans were the founders of the Liao dynasty (907–1125) and the Jin dynasty of China (1125–1222) and others.

Shamanism entered China at an early age and deeply influenced Taoism (and to a lesser extent Confucianism) with its concept of an ideal society associated with matriarchal memories, the Taoist feminine symbol, magic and the emphasis on sex techniques said to have an integral connection with the whole universe – a similar view is held by Tantric Buddhists.

The shamanic cult of nature is found especially in the great poetry of Ch'u Yuan (about 340–278 BCE) who longed to escape from his exile in the south. His 'symbolic escape from the earth by means of ritual ecstasy, calling for the help of nature by chants of priests (and priestesses) rising high above the world of pains in heavenly "distant travels"'.[27]

Korean shamanism

Shamanism is still active in Korea, being deeply rooted in the ethnic consciousness of the people. It exists alongside Buddhism, Confucianism, Taoism and Christianity, which it has also influenced. It is known as *sin'gyo*, the religion of the gods, and includes a bear and a sun cult and ancestor worship, indicating a link with the cultures of Central Asia, Siberia and Manchuria.

Before the time of the Chosŏn dynasty, shamans enjoyed high social standing; some were rulers such as Namhae, the second king of the Silla dynasty (reigned 4–23 CE), but after the advent of the incoming religions many privileges were lost. However, in 1973 there were over 100,000 shamans in South Korea.[28] Formerly they retained their official functions at the royal and national sacrificial rites, until Korea was annexed by Japan in 1910 when the Japanese obliterated as much as they could of the native religion, by raiding the ceremonies, destroying sacrificial offerings and arresting shamans. After liberation in 1945 the shamans came up against hostile Korean Christians who persecuted them and their followers, calling them devotees of the devil. An even worse time for shamanism occurred in Communist North Korea which caused the religion to go underground.

Evenki shamaness

A recent description of a rite of blessing performed by the 90-year-old Evenki shamaness Matrio Petrovna Kurbeltinova (d. 1996) relates that she was assisted by her grandson who prepared a larch to represent the ritual tree up which the souls would travel to the upper world. She put on her special garments and hat and fumigated the place with burnt juniper. Then she appealed to the spirit-helpers to come down to Earth. First came the cuckoo and the hooper (wild swan). The cuckoo is especially sacred, having once been a human being who was turned into a bird by a shaman from the Kukti clan. Meeting a cuckoo in the forest brings luck and happiness. The shamaness has a small stuffed figure of a bear – a vestige of an archaic bear cult. Then she requested good things and influences to come from the nearby river, appealed to Heaven, and to Mother-Elk, her soul and spiritual double. After spinning round at high speed and drumming she finally sat down and started telling the fortunes of the audience.

Today, shamanic ceremonies are much simplified, the sacred places having been destroyed and the traditional shamans' schools no longer in existence. However, since the 1960s shamanism has been much encouraged by the annual National Festival of Folk Art. There has also been more interest in the music, songs and dances associated with the ritual. Some people regard the dances as erratic and disorganized, although in fact specific rules govern each kind of step and one could say that the dances are 'choreographed'. It has been suggested that the ritualized order of the dance increases its power. The sounds of nature can be heard in the songs, refrains are sung by the shaman's assistants who lead the audience and are essential to raise the shaman's soul energy. His body channels were opened by means of the smoke of a sacred plant (*swaih*) to enable soul energy to travel out and spirit energy to come in.

'Manchus believe that hot smoke entering the body can make the inner energy rise up to help the shaman experience the ecstatic journey.'[29]

Lapp shamanism

Today some Laplanders are nomadic, living with their reindeer herds in mountainous regions; others are agriculturists or fishermen. In pre-Christian times the Lapps were shamanists and nature worshippers. They honoured the sun and the moon, had deities among the stars, and underworld demons. Their thunder god was Atja – the name means both 'father' and 'thunder'. They consulted rune trees inscribed with the figures of gods, men and animals. Formerly, they practised polygamy and polyandry.

Christian missionaries fought hard against the Lapps' ancient religion and much of it disappeared, although a strong belief in wizards was retained. The chief of their once rich pantheon of gods is Radien-Atche, who entrusted the work of creation to his son Radien-Kiedde, and his daughter Radien-Nieda.

Shamans and smiths

In many ancient cultures iron was regarded as both mysterious and sacred. As smiths have power over fire, they were believed to be sorcerers and keepers of professional secrets, and therefore Siberian shamans and smiths have hereditary vocations. By the ninth generation a smith acquires supernatural powers, but if he lacks a sufficient number of ancestors and also makes shamanic ornaments, he will be attacked by birds with crooked beaks which will tear his heart to pieces unless the fire surrounds him on all sides. These hereditary shamans are said to have tools that are possessed by spirits and which can make sounds by themselves.[30] Thus when an Altaic shaman descends to the underworld of Erlik Khan, he hears metallic noises.

The archaic magical mastery over fire is seen in the Arctic shaman and in the Hindu ascetic – both are able to resist extremes of heat and cold by means of their own inner heat that enables them to reach higher spiritual planes. In India, when this technique controlling internal heat (*tapas*) has been perfected, it indicates that an unconditioned state of perfect spiritual freedom has been achieved. Power over fire assimilates a number of shamanic feats far beyond the confines of the human condition.

A Yakut proverb states that the first smith, the first shaman and the first potter were blood-brothers. As the smith was the eldest and then the shaman, a shaman cannot cause the death of a smith but a smith may burn a shaman's soul.[31] Another proverb states that smiths and shamans come from the same 'nest'.

Blacksmiths are able to transmute both metals and human lives.

As they are unafraid of the powers of shamans they are able to make the many metal images of spirit-helpers and weapons that adorn the shaman's costume. The noise of the metal objects terrifies hostile spirits during the ritual performance.[32]

Yakut mythology relates that the smith's trade was given to the shaman by the sinister deity K'daai Maqsin, the chief underworld Master Smith of Hell, who dwells in an iron house surrounded by flames. He possesses also curative properties including repairing the broken bones of heroes, as well as tempering the souls of famous shamans even as he tempers iron.[33] Sometimes he joins in the initiation of famous shamans from the supernatural world. Another mythical smith, Chyky, forged the weapons of warriors and gave them wise advice.

The good gods of the Buriats, called the White Tengri, sent down to Earth the celestial smith Boshintoi with his daughter and nine sons who taught human beings the art of metallurgy. (Their first pupils became the ancestors of the later families of smiths.) The smiths sacrificed a horse and tore out its heart. The animal's soul is said to have rejoined the celestial smith. Nine young men play the part of Boshintoi's nine sons, and the man incarnating the heavenly smith falls into a trance and relates how in olden times he sent his son to civilize human beings, then he touches the fire with his tongue. 'Black' smiths are much feared by the people for they are protected by hostile spirits which eat the souls of humans.

The smiths' mysterious art transforms the weapons of heroes into magical instruments, hence epic writings describe the close relationship between smiths and heroes. It is an interesting fact that among many Mongolian and Turkish tribes, the term for 'smith' (*darkhan*) means both 'hero' and 'free horseman'. There is also a Mongolian tradition that Genghis Khan was originally a smith.

In the mythology of many ancient cultures divine smiths forge weapons for the gods. Thus the Vedic Indian divine artisan Tvaṣṭar, the 'shaper or fashioner', is also called the 'earliest born' (*Rigveda* 1, 13, 10). He fashioned the sacrificial ladle and the chalice of the gods. As early as 2500 BCE, the technology of metalworking in India was well established, as attested by the beautiful bronze figures dating from that time. The craftsmen themselves were highly respected members of the community. The bronze religious statues of southern India are believed to radiate the energy of the divine. Certain metals are said to possess healing properties as described in Ayurvedic medicine.

In Delhi there is a famous solid iron pillar, 7.2 metres tall and with a deep base, which dates from about 400 CE. European metallurgists were unable to make such large castings until the nineteenth century. Curiously enough the iron shows no signs of wear or rust – a fact that so far no one can explain.

The Egyptian god Ptah was the god of craftsmen, and the Babylonian Mummu personified technical skill, as did the Phoenician Chusor and the Greek Hephaistos. In Northern mythology, Thor has the sacred hammer which is the thunderbolt. The artisan Koshar forged clubs for Baal which could be hurled great distances.[34]

In all cultures, when weapons were first made, a magic aura was associated with the tools as well as giving the skilled artisan great prestige in the community; thus metallurgy has always been a source of awe. As smiths are able to make shamanistic ritual ornaments they must possess supernatural skills as well as 'peculiar fingers'.

2

Trance, Ecstasy and Possession

Trance, a transcendent state of awareness, constitutes an important part of shamanism. Trance, ecstasy and possession by spirits are the same thing in some forms of shamanizing. Students of religion call ecstasy trance and psychopathologists refer to it as ecstasy. Genuine ecstasy is a psychogenic reaction according to the dictates of the visionary's mind, so expressing the conscious and unconscious desires of the ecstatic shaman. The idea of 'flight', 'riding' and 'speed' with reference to shamans are all figurative expressions for ecstasy, which is controlled throughout the ritual in conformity with traditional prescriptions.

Trance is not a non-conscious state: 'the shaman is in a non-ordinary psychic state which in some cases means not a loss of consciousness but rather an altered state of consciousness'.[1]

The literal Greek term *ekstasis* means to escape from one's own rational and definite position, so in this sense it has the same aim as mysticism, for both transcend the assumed limits of personality. The altered state is entered at will in order to gain knowledge and the power to help others. Furthermore, the shamanic trance does not resemble that of the Western medium who cannot remember what occurred within the trance state.

There are many degrees of trance although the various types tend to merge. In its most extreme form 'it is a conventionalized ritualism in which the shaman's psychomental complex does not differ from that of his common behaviour, thus he is only a "performer"'.[2]

Ecstasy does not always involve the loss of the shaman's soul, since trance states are used also for divination and for healing where no soul loss occurs, and no spiritual journey is undertaken, but he receives useful information from his helping spirits.

When the shaman experiences possession he either invites the spirits to enter him or they themselves seek to enter him. As they are socially approved of these spirits are regarded as benign. Possession always occurs with psychic dissociation when the shaman's own personality becomes submerged. Curiously enough in Christianity this dissociation paves the way for antisocial and antireligious forces in the personality, leading to demonic possession, as in the case of nuns and others during the Middle Ages when the Church succeeded in turning most of Europe into a madhouse.

When experiencing ecstasy the shaman's pulse races, but at the culminating moment of deep trance it is hardly perceptible.[3] Only strong personalities can endure the nervous strain of shamanizing for many hours, although ecstasy gives great strength to the performer. Even old men become agile and shamanesses gain the strength of several grown men. The excitatory mental states resulting from sensory overloading and emotional arousal require great physical and mental exertion by dancing, drumming and singing – such states of high emotion are caught by the audience, and somewhat resemble those of Christian revivalist meetings and the experiences of members of the charismatic churches.

The auto-hypnotic trance state is characterized by dissolving the boundaries of the mundane world in which everyday things are but fragments of existence artificially removed from the wholeness of being and then given 'a relative sense of meaning; entities that do not really exist for us except in a conditioned way'.[4]

Ecstasy allows the shaman to experience primordial time and to reach planes accessible to ordinary people only through death. As a competent shaman can bring about and control ecstasy voluntarily it cannot be classed as a form of epilepsy since an ordinary patient cannot control the illness. Some minor shamans receive the god's commands in dreams, visions or by the use of hallucinogenic mushrooms such as the fly agaric or by narcotics.

When mind-altering drugs are taken, the unconditioned world appears radiant, a fact attested by many individuals who have used such drugs. Everything is experienced simultaneously independently of temporal sequence. Thus time is abolished. (The terror of time is the most damaging of illusions.) All colours are greatly enhanced. Some sub-Arctic shamans induce semi-trances with the help of narcotics or they mime the souls' journey, but Arctic shamans spontaneously achieve the trance state without artificial aids, believing that only less skilled shamans use them.

In Siberia the fly agaric induced ecstatic visions and a feeling of communication with the divine. The curious effects of this powerful drug were the basis of a number of traditional descriptions of the Christian and Islamic heavens. Sometimes alcohol, especially vodka, was used for the same purpose. The shamanic performances usually take place in darkness or semi-darkness which removes the distractions of ordinary reality. Thus the shaman can literally 'see' in darkness things and future events imperceptible to ordinary people.

The Tsingala (Ostyak) shaman offers sacrifices to Sänke, a celestial shining god. Then he eats three mushrooms and falls into a trance. Female shamans use the same method. Songs are sung to Sänke which contain information learned on the shaman's ecstatic journey to the supreme being, for songs penetrate the barrier between human beings and the spirit world. Sometimes the journey occurs during a cataleptic trance when he appears to be dead, his soul having left the body. The distance that the powerful *duńd* (dragonfly) shamans of the Kets could travel in trance depended on the number of helping spirits who were arranged in rows, seven to a row.

Frenzied dancing also causes trance accompanied by increased suggestibility, making the performer immune to all fears. The Greek Maenads, worshippers of Dionysus god of wine, used alcohol and other drugs to achieve 'transformation'. They danced in violent abandon on the mountains accompanied by the persistent heavy beat of the tympanum, the eerie smoky light of torches and their own shrieks and yells. Such intense erotic excitement also contributed to producing the final state of *ekstasis* (standing outside oneself) and *enthousiasmos* (possession by the god). The Maenads saw visions and were endowed with supernatural strength, tearing live animals to pieces and eating the flesh. During the rite the women's personalities were temporally displaced by altered states of consciousness. The animals embodied the god Dionysus, and eating them enabled the eater to add the animal's life to hers and to attain unity with the deity, for 'blood is the life' as the Hebrews believe. According to the Old Testament without the shedding of blood there can be no remission of sins. Thus the essence of the Eucharist was undoubtedly the magical effect ascribed to the bodily communion with Christ by partaking, albeit symbolically, his body and blood.[5]

The ecstatic flight or journey

Such experiences were common to the whole of archaic humanity, but became much changed and modified over the centuries by the different cultures and religions that shamanism encountered. In some cultures it was highly regarded, in others devalued. In most early beliefs the supreme being was always connected with 'height' which itself was regarded as sacred. The supreme gods were called 'He on high', or 'He of the sky', although later the sky gods lost their predominance, but this did not nullify the religious symbolism of ascent. For wherever it is found it denotes the transcending of the human condition to reach higher planes.

Sometimes the shaman uses a ladder with which he ascends to the sky. Gods and dead souls are said to descend to earth by means of ladders. The Egyptian god of the dead states that 'I set up a ladder to heaven among the gods'. A number of amulets in the form of ladders have been found in the tombs of the early dynasties. Jacob dreamed of a ladder reaching Heaven on which angels ascended and descended (Genesis 28. 12). Similarly Mohammad saw a ladder with angels in the Jerusalem temple. It reached to Heaven and by it virtuous souls reached Allah. St John Climaeus symbolized the phases of spiritual ascent by a ladder. Ladder symbolism was also used by some Christian mystics.

The Altaians sometimes perform a horse sacrifice when the shaman is about to ascend to the sky. A new *yurt* is erected in a meadow. A young birch tree is stripped of its lower branches and placed inside. Nine steps are cut into the trunk. A small 'fence' of birch twigs surround the *yurt* and a birch stick with a knot of horsehair on it is placed at the entrance. A light-coloured horse pleasing to the deity is chosen. A man holds the animal's head and the shaman shakes a birch branch over the horse's back to force its soul to leave its body and prepare for the flight to the celestial world of the god Bai Ülgen.

A branch is also shaken over the man holding the horse, thereby enabling his soul to accompany the animal's. The shaman enters the *yurt*, fumigates his drum and invokes his helping spirits to enter it. Each spirit is addressed by name and each replies: 'I am here, *kam!*' The shaman appears to be catching the spirits in his drum and then leaves the *yurt*. Nearby is a figure of a goose made of rags and straw which the shaman straddles and waves his hands as if flying while singing: 'Under the white sky/Over the white cloud/Under the blue sky/Over the blue cloud;/Rise up to the sky, bird!' Whereupon the goose replies, which is of course the shaman himself imitating the bird's cackle. In ancient India and North and Central Asia there were a number of bird cults associated with local deities. In Vedic India the semi-divine goose (*haṁsa*) was closely associated with the sun as it is in shamanism. The bird also represented knowledge and the life force or cosmic breath. The Egyptian sun god Amon Ra flew in the form of a goose over the primordial waters and its honking was the first sound ever made.[6] Similarly 'the Spirit of God moved upon the face of the waters' (Genesis 1. 2).

The shaman pursues the soul of the horse which is supposed to have fled. With the help of the audience he drives the horse's soul into the fenced area and mimes its capture. He blesses the animal and kills it, again with the help of the assembly, by breaking its backbone and without a drop of blood falling on the ground or on to the sacrificer. The skin and bones are hung up on a long pole and an offering is made to the ancestors and tutelary spirits of the *yurt*. The flesh is eaten ceremonially. The next evening the most important part of the ceremony is performed. The shaman offers horse meat to the Masters of the Drum, that is, to the spirits personifying the shamanic powers of his family. He sings and also addresses the Masters of Fire, eats the meat and distributes some to the assembly. Then, as an offering to Bai Ülgen, he fumigates nine garments hung up on a rope which are donated by the owner of the *yurt*. The shaman sings, calling on many spirits and the members of Bai Ülgen's family. Finally, he invokes Markut, the mythical Bird of Heaven. He imitates its cry and drops one shoulder as if under the weight of the great bird. Then purifying the assembly with the drum he becomes increasingly ecstatic and begins his celestial ascent, starting at the first notch in the birch tree trunk. The tree represents the World Tree situated at the centre of the universe; it functions as the cosmic axis connecting sky, Earth and underworld. The notches denote the various celestial planes.

The shaman circles the birch and the fire imitating thunder and then mounts a bench covered with horse hide representing the soul of the sacrificed horse. The horse enables the shaman 'to come out of himself', so making his magical flight to the heavens possible, but by the time the first heaven is reached the horse tires and the goose is summoned to take its place as the shaman continues his spiritual journey, after he has prophesied concerning the state of the coming weather and the future dangers that threaten the community. In the sixth heaven a hare hunt takes place – the hare being a lunar animal, it is hunted in the sixth heaven of the moon. The sun is in the seventh heaven. The shaman reaches the ninth heaven but a really great shaman may reach the twelfth or even higher. The shaman respectfully addresses Bai Ülgen who gives him information concerning the state of the coming harvest after which he collapses totally and remains motionless. After a time he wakes as if from a deep sleep and greets the assembled people.[7]

The visions and motifs seen by the shaman are repeated in his songs describing the various spirits he calls up and their journey to the ritual performance. During singing his ecstasy increases. Some songs, such as those of the Nenets, are often improvised. The rhythmical drumming, apart from the singing, is enough to cause changes in the electrical activity of the brain in ordinary people.

A number of Christian saints while in trance are reported to have remained suspended in the air for some time. St Teresa (1515–1582) was said to have gone into a state of ecstatic rapture, which felt like being immersed in a soft cloud, or carried away by a giant eagle. During this time it was necessary for the nuns to sit on her to keep her from floating off the Earth! St Joseph of Copertino (1603–1663) often flew seven or eight feet off the ground in order to kiss the figure of the holy infant on the altar. One day he even carried up another friar and floated around the room with him. One of the central motifs of the hero tales having shamanistic elements is the hero's flight to the other world on the back of a mythical bird which he then feeds with bits of his own flesh.

It has been pointed out that there is no definite psychological state that can be identified with 'trance', nor can its presence be proved or disproved, yet it may be experienced by seers, diviners, lamas, hunters and others.[8] However, Western writers have greatly sensationalized the more exotic aspects of shamanism, even as they overemphasized the sexual part of Tibetan tantrism.

Descent to the underworld

Few shamans are capable of descending to the underworld; it is usually the speciality of 'Black shamans' who are able to deal with powerful hostile spirits and demonic influences. However, whether the shaman is ascending or descending, his soul leaves his body. Accompanied by his helping spirits and the souls of his ancestors he makes a vertical descent from the Earth through seven successive subterranean levels or regions called 'obstacles' (*pudak*). Curious metallic sounds are heard in these regions including the sounds of waves and gales, until finally he reaches the seventh level, the source of the nine underworld rivers. Here is situated the heavily defended stone and black clay palace of Erlik, ruler of the dead. Dogs guard the palace and its domains. These dogs are reminiscent of the Greek Cerberus and the Indic Sārameyas who guard the way to the dead. Goldi shamans cannot undertake the subterranean journey without the bird spirit that ensures their safe return to earth. Eliade suggests that Erlik's underworld is based on an Irano-Indian model.[9]

The underworld is regarded as an inverted image of this world; thus the rivers flow back to their source, grave offerings are placed upside down so they will be the right way up in the underworld; or, if broken, will become intact again. The Siberian Tatars have seven or nine underground regions, and the Samoyeds have six situated under the sea.

During the underworld journey the shaman often appears to be dead. An Alaskan shaman related that he had been dead for two days, during which time he traversed the well-trodden path of the dead and heard the weeping and wailing of the living. Finally he came to a village where two shades took him into a house where a bright fire was burning with meat in a pot boiling on it. He was warned not to eat the meat; otherwise he would be unable to return to earth. He resumed his journey, finally coming down to his own grave, whereupon he re-entered his body which came back to life. Then he returned to his village and recounted his adventures.[10]

Some Altaic shamans escort the soul to the underworld but in order not to be recognized by the dead they put soot on their faces. (The black garments worn by Christians were *de rigueur* for mourners up to the 1950s and based originally on a similar idea that demons would not see them.)

The horse in many cultures has a funerary aspect. It is the mythical image of death, and hence it is incorporated into archaic ecstatic techniques. The horse leads or carries the dead into the next world. The horse of the ancient Indian horse sacrifice led the way to the sun. Ancient Greek heroes were also associated with horses which were depicted on their graves. In the history of religions, various types of descent to the underworld are known, including those of Ishtar, Herakles and Jesus.

Eliade maintains that the increasingly important role of the ancestor cult and the divine figures that took the place of the supreme being have altered the meaning of the shaman's experience. The descent into the underworld, hostile spirits and possession are mostly recent innovations. Furthermore, there are other influences to be considered including the various effects of Tibetan Buddhism, of the Tibetan animistic Bon religion, of Indian, Iranian and lastly the 'Mesopotamian influences that preceded them'.[11]

Ecstatic religions

The Old Germanic religion included vestiges of archaic shamanistic practices, especially in Odin's acquisition of runic knowledge, poetic art and magic achieved through his own self-sacrifice. Odin is also 'the god of cult ecstasy . . . and the Berserk fury bears all the traits of ecstatic states of consciousness, insensitivity to fire and pain (as well as not bleeding) a phenomena known from shamanic trances'.[12] Similarly, Baldr passes through a shamanistic type of initiation in which he experiences death, and a journey to the other world. Christ also died for three days and then was resurrected but he did not remain on Earth.

So deep were the trances experienced by Odin's warriors – the Berserkers and the Wolfskins – that they felt no pain. Both belonged 'to the type of warrior in animal guise, who had their origin in the cult bands of [masked] warriors of German antiquity, dedicated to Odin'.[13] Their battle fury or Berserk-fury was so powerful that they became invulnerable as they roared into battle.

Odin is associated with extraordinary altered states of consciousness associated with magic and with his role as leader of the Wild Hunt. He views the whole Earth from his high seat. This somewhat resembles the platforms used by shamans when experiencing their visions. The ancient German seeresses also used similar constructions.

The inspired Hebrew prophets claimed their ecstatic words came to them from Yahweh who caused an evil spirit to enter Saul, making him prophesy ecstatically (or 'to rave' – this is the alternative reading of 1 Samuel 18. 10; see also 1 Kings 22f.). In his frenzy Saul stripped off his clothes and lay naked for a day and a night. By means of the sacred frenzy Yahweh possesses the individual who then becomes his agent for good or evil purposes. According to the Old Testament some professional diviners gave oracular responses while in a state of trance. Elijah's trance was induced by bowing down to the Earth and putting his face between his knees (1 Kings 18. 42; Balaam, when in trance, actually heard Yahweh's words). In the New Testament Paul gained knowledge of future events.

Ecstatic states are also experienced by Dervishes and formerly by medieval mystics and by the Finnish trance-preachers. Ancient sources report similar phenomena among the West Semitic population of Mari during the nineteenth and eighteenth centuries BCE and also among Phoenicians and Canaanites. Ecstasy is also a feature of romantic love both in Europe and Oriental literature, and appears to have an archaic root.

Rohde saw a connection between ancient Greek religion, especially the Bacchanalianism of Thrace, and shamanism.[14] Furthermore, he linked the Thracian cult of ecstasy and the use of smoke to the Pontic steppe and to Asia. The Greeks regarded the state of ecstasy accompanied by hallucination, insensibility to pain or to ordinary sensations as a sign of union with God.

When a chant unites with the vibrations of a drum it is the classic shaman's power chant that frees the superconscious from ordinary consciousness.[15] With the expansion of consciousness, the ego unites with the rest of the world, gives heightened sensitivity to all modalities of the senses and dissolves the limiting boundary between the individual ego and the world. The experience of the slowing down of time, or even of its abolition, is an essential part of trance. We all long for ego-loss which is sought in passionate love, dancing, singing, pop music and intoxicants or drugs.

It has been shown that if drum rhythm is synchronized with brainwave frequencies, an altered state of consciousness is more easily achieved. Essentially there is no distinction between trance and deep hypnosis.[16] Aldous Huxley pointed out years ago that all our experiences are chemically conditioned, whether we think of them as 'spiritual', 'aesthetic' or purely 'intellectual'.[17] Trance states can also result from oxygen deficiency.

William Sargant has drawn attention to the irrationality of the ecstatic forms of worship that existed in the early church, and emphasizes that it is the brain in man and not his soul that is affected by mystical techniques.

Forms of possession

It is interesting that the so-called possessing spirit or deity is always one associated with his or her own religious background; thus Marie of the Incarnation described how her soul experienced being in union with Him: 'I am in God, possessed by God.'[18] Psychologically, possession implies the domination of the individual personality by 'super'natural powers either good or bad. Possession appears to be real because of the individual's subconscious attitude of expectancy. This explains possession by onlookers as being non-volitional. The God of the Old Testament is said to be surrounded by hosts of spirits (1 Kings 22. 19ff.) who do his bidding for good or evil purposes, the spirits themselves being ethically 'neutral', becoming beneficent or maleficent according to the tasks assigned to them. In the New Testament, Luke (11. 20) claims that the subjugation of evil spirits was one of the chief signs that the Kingdom of God was at hand. He relates the story of Jesus removing many evil spirits from a possessed man. When the spirits saw Jesus they begged him not to cast them into the abyss, but to let them enter a neighbouring herd of swine. Jesus agreed, whereupon the possessed animals rushed headlong over a cliff to their deaths. St Paul too was much occupied with the impending end of the world and with the prevalence of demons which he claimed constituted the greatest hindrances that Christians have to contend with. To him the planetary Archontes were the demonic spirits ruling the world. Their hold on mankind could be broken only by a transcendental deity who was God in whom all good spirits are concentrated.[19] St Paul himself was caught up to the 'third heaven'. Souls ascending 'to the seven heavens – whether during initiation or after death – had tremendous vogue during the last centuries of the pre-Christian era'.[20] Christians may be possessed by God, or by his adversary, the Devil. The same physiological experiences also underlie feelings of union with God, oracular utterances, mediums, and the behaviour of hypnotized persons, or those under the influence of certain drugs, or in states of sexual excitement. Exactly the same mechanism in other cultures produces feelings of possession by Allah, Dionysus, Seraphis, Zeus, Shango the African god of thunder, and so on. In Ethiopia, which is a Christian country, there are many spirits called Satans, who may be good or evil; elsewhere in parts of Africa they are known as Zars or Pepos. Japan has its numerous fox spirits and other supernatural beings. Every religious system has its spirits which makes it impossible to know if any, or all, of these supposed entities are real, and, if some, which ones?

The Ainu shamans of Japan fall into trance in order to cure patients and to discover from whence the disease comes. They also prophesy as the mouthpieces of the gods.[21]

3

Shamans' Paraphernalia

All the paraphernalia, including the costume and every figure depicted on it, is related to shamanic cosmology and beliefs. For example, the most important object is the drum which symbolizes the universe as well as countless other things. Its symbolism is of great complexity as well as including many archaic elements. Unfortunately much of it is known only to believers. Although its origin is unknown some ethnologists consider that the drum came from South Asia. It appears that the Tibetan Buddhist double drum influenced the shape of Siberian, Chukchi and Inuit drums, although similarities have also been noticed between the Tibetan Bon priests' regalia and drum and those of Siberian shamans, such as eagle feathers, a beribboned helmet and various weapons. However, Koppers does not consider that the prototype was Tibetan. Instead, he sees that it is similar in shape to the winnowing baskets found among the archaic peoples of India – the Santal, Bhil and Baiga.[1] Krader has pointed out the shaman's messages, visions and paraphernalia 'are the techniques of a distinctive social role and cult, philosophy, psychology and morality'.[2] In ancient times the drum turned into a 'wild animal' but later with the transition to livestock raising it became a 'horse'.

The rhythm of the drum excites the shaman, as well as controlling the psychic state of the audience. Some shamans possess a number of costumes, drums and other accessories that are determined by the ethnical complex involved. Without the necessary accessories the shaman could not enter the underworld.

Some shamans used Jews' harps, ancient bronze mirrors and fans. During the 1930s and 1940s the famous healing shaman Sonam Tsarin (who was also a blacksmith) performed his rites with an iron Jews' harp with a figure of a horse etched on the handle.

The drum is important in Siberian shamanism as it functions symbolically as a 'horse' for the shaman and, when beaten rhythmically, transports him to the centre of the world, the place of the Cosmic Tree that unites the celestial world with the Earth and with the supreme being, who causes a branch to fall from the tree for the shaman to make the shell of his drum. Siberian shamans have their own sacred trees representing the Cosmic Tree. Some use trees planted with their roots in the air. This is one of the most archaic symbols of the World Tree. The 'inverted tree' was known in Babylonia and in India. The ancient Vedic text the *Rigveda* (1. 24. 7) refers to a tree whose roots are on high; the *Kaṭha-Upaniṣad* (VI. I) refers to the aśvattha tree (*Ficus religiosa*) as the eternal Tree of Life whose roots are in heaven, that is, in the divine essence, the impersonal *brahman*, and so represents creation as a descending movement from above.[3]

Yakuts prefer to use a tree that has been struck by lightning, probably because lightning comes from the celestial world. In some contexts lightning is regarded as the anger of the gods. An Altaic shaman related how the tree was cut, and the way it was taken to the village. He gives details of the animal's birth (whose hide makes the drum), its parents and its life until it was hunted down, so both the shell and the skin of the drum contain magico-religious elements which enable the visionary to undertake his ecstatic journey. The drum animal is the shaman's chief spirit or *alter-ego*.

Before being used ritually the drum has to be 'reanimated' or 'enlivened' by daubing it with blood, beer or vodka. By means of the reanimated skin of the drum he 'reanimates' his chief helping animal. When 'it enters the shaman he changes into the mythical theriomorphic ancestor . . . the primordial animal that is the origin of his tribe'.[4]

The idea of the drum as a saddle animal is of great antiquity. It originated in the hunting area of the mountainous *taiga* region.

The southern drum is large, oval and is held by four loose bands fastened to the hoop on the inner side. The other ends of the bands meet in the middle and are tied to a small wheel or cross. When held, the drum hangs loosely and its position may be changed easily. Most drums are made with the skin of reindeer, elk or horse hide and have designs on them including human and animal figures and other symbols, but Ostyak and Samoyed drums have no designs.[5] The Chukchi drum has a very thin skin, usually made of the dried skin of a walrus stomach.

Among the Koryaks, the oval drum belongs to the family and not to the shaman. It is both a musical instrument and a sacred object. It is covered with reindeer hide on one side only, the whalebone drumstick is wider at the end which strikes the drum and it is covered with the skin of a wolf's tail. A snake depicted on a Tuvan drumstick represents the shaman's 'whip' with which he urges on his mount, as well as using it to defend himself against hostile forces. A rider on a goat depicted on a drumstick indicates that the shaman is travelling on his ecstatic journey.

Yukaghir and Yakut drums are similar in shape including the small protruberances on the outer rims said to be the horns of the shaman's spirits. The drumstick is covered with skin taken from the shaman's own leg. The Yukaghir term for the drum is *yalgil* meaning 'lake', that is, the lake into which the shaman dives to reach the shadow world. (To have a drum (*yalgi'ne*) also means 'to shamanize'.)

Drum decorations

The Transbaikal Tungus drums depict birds, snakes and other animals as well as human figures. The centre of the instrument is left undecorated except for eight double lines symbolizing the eight supports that hold the Earth above the waters.[6] Rattles, bells and iron figurines represent various spirits and animals, as well as magical weapons such as bows or knives, but unfortunately much of this symbolism is only fully understood by initiates. The drums of the Ugrian peoples are undecorated.

Drumming and rhythm produces a physiological and psychic state in which the spirit speaks; that is, the shaman himself makes a suggestion which immediately 'doubles' the effect of the drumming. The audience enter into the performance by singing and keeping up the rhythm.

Altaic and Mongolian drums have similar decorations, but with a horizontal line across the centre dividing the two worlds above and below. A birch tree is depicted on the lower part – an allusion to the trees surrounding the place where animal sacrifices are held and the two trees that grow in Ulukhan's country. Also the black and white frogs that serve Ulukhan and the spirits associated with seven nests and seven feathers, the bringers of disease to humans. Ülgere is prayed to to cure earache and toothache, and also Ot-imeze, the Mother of Fire. On the upper part are the sun and two blackbirds, messengers from the south to the black spirit, a bear's tooth and Ulukhan's horses. Other white figures represent the animals that Kyzyl-kikh-khan hunts. He is prayed to before any undertaking.[7]

Various animals are depicted on Turkic drums called *buras* or *burgas* which function as saddle animals for the Earth spirits and for the shaman himself. The first animal (*bura*) on a Teleut drum belongs to the owner of the drum and represents his soul animal, and hence is linked closely to his life. If his *bura* is taken from him he can no longer shamanize and death soon follows. Because of the dangers associated with losing the drum, it is kept hidden from other shamans and also from hostile spirits. The special *bura* is either all white or red-dotted white; that is, 'a spotted horse'.[8]

Teleut drums had the most *bura* images and were the horses belonging to various deities. Each clan deity rode a horse of a specific colour. Thus the Yuth clan's *bura* was a pale reddish yellow; the Mundu's was black; the Merkit's light olive brown, and so on. These *buras* establish the Teleut and Shor clans' compositions. Similarly, the Kachins and Sagais claim that the mountain spirits of the Sayan range rode horses of different colours, but unicoloured horses were sacrificed to a specific divinity. The Teleut god Ülgen had a roan horse, the mountain spirit a sorrel. (The Teleut and Shor peoples bred only skewbald horses.) Some Teleut drums depict 'secondary spirits' belonging to the earth spirits which are also white; the numbers vary from shaman to shaman.

A long-legged frog is depicted on the lower parts of Baraba drums. To the Teleuts, Shors and Kumandins the frog is regarded as the shaman's assistant as well as accompanying him on his wanderings. When a Kumandin shaman sacrifices to Ülgen, the birch-bark vessel is carried by the frog (*paya*) spirit up to the patron clan spirit. The vessel is full of a kind of beer used in sacrifices. The frog's leg acts as a stopper if a leak occurs during a ritual. The Shors claim that the mighty frog was received by the shaman from the supreme being. On Shor drums, the frog has six legs. Frog figures are also put on the coats of Altai Kizhi shamans, but not on their drums.

It has been suggested that vestiges of the ancient clan cult connected with independent animal worship stem from the time when the clan had its own patron animal and hence it was represented on their drums. But when the clan cult ceased to be practised the clan's shaman also acted for several other clans causing the degeneration of the original clan's tradition. Thus when other clans used the drum for shamanizing they depicted their own sacred animals on it.[9]

Before shamanizing in honour of a certain spirit its 'horse' has to be captured and tethered, otherwise the spirit may be out riding its own *bura*. Erlik's *bura* is guarded by Porüchi Khan, so before the shaman can carry out the performance he undergoes a special rite that enables him to seize Erlik's 'horse' from Porüchi.

The shaman's saddle animal is usually represented as horned so it may be an elk, moose or reindeer. Altai Kizhi drums show a ram-like animal with three long horns. Each drum always has three *buras*.

The mighty birch tree, the chief of trees, has an important role among the Shors, so the drum handle is made of birch and also the wooden parts of the sacrificial altar dedicated to the higher spirits. The great birch connects Heaven and Earth and the shaman climbs up its nine rings to the nearest clouds, then on to the top of the birch which lies far beyond the clouds. It is connected to Heaven by two parallel silk threads up which the shaman climbs. The top of the tree is covered eternally with snow. If the shaman knocks a branch snow falls to Earth. The tree stands beyond the imaginary 'milk lake' in the east; or it grows on high mountains.

The Siberian Chulym Turks had no special costume for shamanizing, although it was necessary to wear iron-shod boots to summon or to drive away spirits by stamping the feet. The shaman wore a piece of cloth knotted around his head with the knot resting on his forehead and the two ends covering his eyes. The cloth itself had an independent part in the rite. With it the spirits were called up. When the shaman's hands were occupied, the cloth was placed on his left shoulder, because he communicated with spirits on his left. Old women waved similar cloths to ward away hostile spirits. The Chulyms use a sacred rattle during the ceremony instead of a drum. The rattle was made from a curved piece of birch root with a wire attached to it with nine metal rings. There are perhaps up to sixty rings according to the strength of the shaman who owns it. The main purpose of the spoon-shaped birch drumstick was to feed the hostile spirits with meat soup and intoxicants. (The spoon was also used for divinatory purposes.)

Ket drum-making ceremony

The Kets' drum-making ceremony shows that the instrument was regarded as a living being, therefore a scraper was never used to remove the deer's hair from the skin intended for the drum head, for this would harm the animal; the hoop and handle were cut from an unfelled tree and all splinters were gathered up and taken to the woods, where they were 'poured into a hollow on the eastern side of the tree' (a characteristic ritual related to the idea of enlivening).[10] South Siberian Turks and Selkups believe that a shaman's life depends on the condition of his drum as well as on the rite of 'enlivening' it, usually by sprinkling it with alcohol.

Although differences exist in the shamanisms of the Siberian peoples, all regard the drum as representing the whole Earth, thus the shaman is closely connected with the cosmos and with cosmic rhythms. The 'centre' is always marked on Siberian drums; the centre of Evenki drums is called the 'road' and the hole in the middle 'the navel of the world'.

A Khakas man stated that the vertical line crossing the leather of the drum served for orientation when one is in unknown territory. Evenki drums are orientated to the north by shamans. The Pleiades are represented on Nganasan drums in the form of holes, which when looked through served as orientation. However, the zealous Christian priests burned hundreds of drums, although they were told that they were used as compasses.[11]

Helping spirits are depicted on Chelkan drums in human form, or as a mountain goat or elk. Some drum handles are in human form and may represent the shaman's Master spirit. Nanai, Udegei and Negidal drums depict a snake-pair supporting the earth. The Great Bear, Orion and the Pleiades are pictured on the upper part of Khakas and Teleut drums, with stars between them; Selkup drums have a lizard and World Tree.

When a Tuvan shaman beats the lower part of his drum it represents the underworld and indicates that he is speaking to Erlik; when beating the upper part he speaks to Ülgen, god of heaven. Thus 'the handle of the Tuvan drum is a copy of the universe personified as a twin deity'.[12] Kachin drums had spirits depicted on them in the shapes of a cuckoo, black or white birds, wolf, bear, dog, elk, chamois, pike, frogs, snakes, lizards or people mounted on red or black horses.

Lapp, Sāmi and Tatar drums

The Lapps use their drums for divinatory purposes, as do the Tungus who perform a simple method of divination by throwing the drumstick into the air. Its position after falling provides answers to the questions asked. Tungus drums are cut from a living larch tree, which is left alive in honour of the Tuuri tree. Lapp drums are covered with images including the World Tree, sun and moon, rainbow, the sacrificial horse, the underworld of Erlik with his seven sons and seven daughters and so on. Usually three cosmic zones or planes are depicted – the sky, Earth, underworld – through which the shaman travels. The concept of three zones is a 'notion rooted in the way of thinking of the Palaeolithic hunters'.[13]

The Scandinavian shamanic drums were one of the most important elements in ecstatic techniques (and for divinatory purposes) of the northern Eurasian peoples. The drum was used until the latter half of the nineteenth century, when finally the Christian missionaries systematically destroyed many of them, but fortunately the Sāmi people hid some of their instruments which are now on display in the Nordic Folk Museum, Stockholm. Symbolic figures were carved on the drums and outlined in blood. It was necessary for the drum-makers to have a knowledge of shamanism and its symbols, and some of them may have been shamans.

Sāmi and Tatar drums are much more decorative than those of other North European peoples. The meanings of the symbols are interpreted by the shaman during his ritual performance. Small metal triangular objects are placed on the drum which are interpreted according to their position in relation to the figures and lines on the instrument. The figures include men hunting, men sitting in boats, mythological beings, graves, mountains, lakes, reindeer or moose, trees, traps, weapons, foxes, polecats, pine martens, squirrels and various birds.

The drums were stored in the holiest corner of the Lapp tent; women were not allowed to touch them.

Mirrors

Symbolic meaning is attached to all the shaman's accessories. All the objects connected with the shaman are sacred because of their contacts with him and with supernatural powers. They are charged also with psychic power and hence are highly dangerous to the uninitiated. Similarly, the Hebrews regarded Mount Sinai, God's abode, as so holy that it was fatal for anyone to go on it or even to touch its borders (Exodus 19. 12f., 21ff.). In the same work (33. 20, 23) God said: 'You cannot see my face for there shall no man see me and live, but you shall see my backparts.' The concept of holiness originally had nothing to do with morality or ethics, but with the supposed relationship of certain individuals, magicians, animals, places and things to the supernatural which set them apart from mundane and non-holy persons and objects.[14]

The Nanai metal mirrors (*toli*) show Sino-Manchurian influences. As early as the second millennium BCE such mirrors were widespread throughout southern Siberia. They reflect the clan's good or bad deeds, as well as protecting the shaman, when shamanizing, from the arrows of enemies, for his spirit-helper dwells in the mirror. The latter is also a receptacle for the soul or the spirit.

Some recordings made in the early 1970s by Kile Polokto show that the discs or mirrors were believed to accommodate the spirits of dogs used by shamans to carry dead souls to the next world. Dogs are associated with the dead in a number of cultures including the Vedic Sārameyas who guard the road to the world of the dead, and the Greek Cerberus. A shaman explained that the disc accommodated the harnessed lead-dog and the other dogs which after a great feast 'took the *mudge* dolls, which were receptacles of the souls of the dead, to the world beyond'.[15] To treat a patient, the Nanai shaman puts a spirit-causing entity into the metal disc in the form of a wooden anthropomorphic or zoomorphic figurine of the spirit and then places the disc on the diseased area.

Some Tungus see the mirror as a receptacle for the 'soul-shade' so the shaman can see a dead person's soul. Some Mongolian shamans see the sacred white horse of the shamans reflected in it. This is the horse by which they achieve their ecstatic flights. Such shamans also have iron mirrors hanging from their belts which represent their individual horses.[16]

Ancient bronze mirrors are the most powerful spirit protectors of a Tuvan shaman. A Chinese brass mirror with pendants attached is used by a Tungus shaman; in this mirror he sees 'everything' including the 'other world'. The mirror focuses his mind. The Birarčens regard it as an important placing for spirits; the Goldi people believe that all human deeds are reflected in it. They also use it for self-protection against the arrows of hostile spirits.

Great powers were attributed to the mirrors. They could purify water, frighten away hostile spirits, avert disease and suffering, contain or replace the soul or be used for divination. On the backs of the heavy bronze mirrors the twelve animals of the time cycle may be depicted or the Chinese Buddhist 'eternal knot'. The more mirrors a shaman has the greater his wisdom and intelligence, for all kinds of things are acquired through the mirrors including 'natural things, the sun, moon and stars, all are absorbed into your body'.[17]

Among the Gilyak and the Olchi the drum and girdle were the most important parts of the shaman's accessories. The girdle was made of heavy leather with many iron and copper hoops and metal pendants which make a loud noise during performances. The chief pendant was a large copper disc ornamented in relief showing Manchu influence.[18]

Shaman's staff

A Tungus shaman's staff may be horse-headed or reindeer-headed with a number of metal rings attached; it is used when dealing with the spirits of the upper world. The shamanic staffs of the Yakuts, Dolgans and Tuvans are surmounted by a carved human head that represents their ancestors.

Sometimes among the Daur, Buriat and Darhat Mongols a staff was used instead of a drum, which was seen to possess magical movement. Thus the Buriat staffs variously represent a 'horse,' a 'snake' or a human being, each one being used for a specific type of journey; or as signs of authority and mastery; or as weapons to punish offenders.

4

Deities and Spirits

Enormous numbers of spirits are known to the various types of shamanism. Over the generations more spirits are added and some others may be forgotten. There is no fixed number, nor are their characters fixed, because shamanism is not a dogmatic religion as are those religions based on sacred texts and revelation.

Shamanic spirits originate in the prehistoric world of nomad hunters and gatherers, whose culture was dominated by animals and bird-like beings. The main helping spirits are the loon, eagle, bear, reindeer and sturgeon. In both Siberia and North America the loon is a mysterious bird which appears in many myths. Sometimes the chief spirit dwelling in the shaman is that of his ancestor, or of a deceased predecessor. Spirits are said to choose a person destined to be a shaman and may leave a special mark on him that comes from the god Ülgen. Both spirits and other supernatural forces worshipped by human beings are regarded as concrete entities.

The Arctic peoples have many taboos concerning a class of 'monsters', the chief of which is the killer-whale. Anyone who kills a whale is certain to die soon afterwards. In winter these mythological whales become wolves and prey on the Chukchi reindeer. There are also other 'monstrous' animals including polar bears, worms, black beetles, birds and fish.[1] The terrors of the world of nature 'are reflected in the [Chukchi] shaman's psychic world of spirits'.[2]

The Chukchi cosmos has five, seven or nine worlds situated one above the other and reached through a hole under the Pole Star. Shamans and spirits travel to these worlds. Some stars constitute distinct worlds with their own inhabitants. The sky is a world that touches our earth at the horizon where there are four gates, from which when opened the winds come rushing out.

There are three main classes of Chukchi spirits. First, invisible ones that bring disease and death and wander the world looking for victims; their faces are strange, some having only one eye. Deformed animals are sacrificed to them. The second are bloodthirsty cannibal spirits, especially dangerous to warriors since ordinary weapons are useless against them. These spirits were originally a tribe of giants living on the Arctic shore who were much troubled by the Chukchi, so they transformed themselves into invisible spirits. The third class of spirits may appear as plants, trees, animals, icebergs and so on. Their tempers are short and they can easily change shape so they must be treated carefully.

Altaians and the Baraba Turks offered animal fur or birds' claws to drum-shaped figures of deities.[3] Erlik is worshipped as god of the underworld 'by all the Altaic Sayan, Turkic-speaking ethnic groups and the Mongolian nationalities'.[4] It is mentioned in the ancient Turkic runic inscriptions of southern Siberia. The chief protective spirit of the Altaians, Katchins and Tuvans is that of the ancestral mountain.

The triple division of the cosmology and of man according to Buriat belief is organized in the same way as their own society; that is, as high-born, commoner and slave. Similarly, the spirits are divided into high, middle and low. The two lower ranks function as intermediaries between man and the highest being; middle-ranking spirits are those of commoners, who also serve the shaman. The spirits of slaves form the lowest class. Human beings are also considered to be composed of three parts: the body, physical organism and the breath animating the whole. The soul of a human being is also divided into three – upper, middle and lower. The ancestral spirit of the clan may descend through males or females, although the Buriat genealogical system is usually patrilineal.[5]

According to Buriat tradition at first there were only good and bad spirits. Then the gods created human beings who lived happily until the hostile gods of the East sent disease and death to the Earth. But some gods decided to help the humans, so they sent them an eagle as a shaman, but the people could not understand the bird so it returned to the gods who then commanded it to return to Earth and grant the gift of shamanizing to the first person seen. This happened to be a woman asleep under a tree, whereupon the eagle had intercourse with her. After this experience the woman saw spirits and became a famous shamaness. Thus an eagle symbolizes the shamanic vocation. Sometimes the supreme being is represented as an eagle perched on the Cosmic Tree on which hang the souls of future shamans. The bird is also relevant to the shaman's costume that transforms him symbolically into an eagle.

When the future shaman is able to have 'spirit visions', it indicates that he has transcended the profane condition of ordinary humans, and henceforth will be able to talk to gods and spirits, although he is able to control only some of them.

A number of great gods are invoked in the ceremonies including Jajyk Kan (Lord of the Sea), Kaira Kan, Bai Ülgen and other mythical beings. A Buriat shaman can function only if his powers are recognized by his own social group, who also pay for his training, costume, paraphernalia and the gifts of his nine cult idols (*ongons*). He is usually unwilling to become a shaman as they are both hated yet needed by their community. But up until the seventeenth century Buriats lived by communal hunting directed by the shaman who was both a lay and spiritual leader. But if a shaman is suspected of witchcraft he will be killed. Male and female shamans are divided into black and white. The former deal with the underworld from which the sun rises, the latter are orientated to the upper world of the West where the sun sets.

Spirits play an important part in initiations and also cause ecstatic states; other divine and semi-divine beings who differ from the shaman's own guardian spirits also assist him. The majority of these spirits have animal or bird forms, but may also appear as phantoms, or as nature or hearth spirits. The usual number of 'familiar' spirits is seven, apart from the 'spirit of the head' which defends him on his ecstatic journeys; a bear-shaped spirit accompanies him on his descent to the underworld, and he mounts to the skies on a grey horse. The greater the number of spirits possessed by a shaman, the greater his power and vice versa. The number of spirits has accumulated over the generations and traditionally the spirits are transmitted to new shamans.

When a Tuva shaman wishes to curse an enemy he imitates the cry of a raven; to call up rain, the cow; to frighten people, the wolf or eagle owl; to uncover a lie, the magpie; to demonstrate his power, the bull; and when expressing rapture, the bear.

Spirits often manifest themselves by the shaman uttering animal cries. The Tungus shaman, whose helping spirit is a snake, imitates the reptile's movements, and Chukchi and Inuit shamans symbolically transform themselves into wolves, bears, reindeer or fish. Or they may don masks to achieve similar results, so emphasizing the fact that the ordinary human condition has been left behind.

From prehistoric times animals in many cultures have been thought to accompany the human soul to the next world. Sajtāns are objects well disposed towards humans because of the 'Master' spirit living in them. All attributes of shamans are called sajtāns, but not until they have been 'spiritualized' by the shaman. On journeys, sajtāns are carried in small round boxes covered with wild deerskin on carts pulled by a spotted or white reindeer – such animals being sacred to shamans. In winter the boxes are put on sledges together with family possessions, except anything belonging to women, for they are unclean. The special reindeer pulling the sajtāns wear a bead-studded tufted bridle. The satjans are inherited by the youngest children of the family.

Bear shamans were protected by the spirit Kojeś who lived on Earth. They were associated with the main Earth Spirit living in the Navel of the Universe. The Earth Spirit provided shamans with spirit-helpers including a female creature that lived in a grove of larches where the shaman's spirit could hide between trances, and where most of his paraphernalia was symbolically preserved.

Vairgit spirits

Benevolent supernatural spirits are called 'beings' (*vairgit*). A special *vairgit* is the sun represented as a man dressed in bright clothes driving dogs or reindeer. The moon is also depicted as a man who carries a lasso with which to catch people who stare fixedly at him. The moon is invoked by shamans with incantations and spells. The Reindeer Chukchi have many 'beings' or spirits as well as a special Reindeer Being (*qoren vairgit*) who watches over the herds; the Maritime people have 'Sea Beings' (*anqa-vairgit*) the most important being Keretkun and his wife who live in a large floating house. Their faces are black and their headgear consists of peculiarly shaped headbands and long white garments made of walrus gut decorated with many small tassels. There are also some walrus-like creatures including the two-tusked 'Mother of the Walrus' who lives at the bottom of the sea. Even the winds are regarded as spirits and invoked in incantations, the local prevailing wind being the chief of these spirits. There are also tent and house spirits who receive small portions of important sacrifices. Other spirits exist including those of hallucinogenic mushrooms.

All forests, trees, waters and animals have spirits or 'Masters' by whom they are animated. In other words these trees, animals, etc. are vessels in which the spirits dwell. Both spirits and animals can assume human form; sometimes the owl and the ermine become warriors. Although animals can impersonate humans they retain some of their animal qualities, so the Fox-woman has a pungent smell, and the Goose-woman does not eat animal food.[6] There are similarities with the ubiquitous Fox-spirits of old Japan.

In some Buriat regions, the protector spirit of shamans is Daian Derkhe whose shrine in northern Mongolia has a specific stone that is said to embody him. Now he protects ancestors and childbirth. The Buriats have fifty-five good western spirits and forty-four evil eastern ones. Mountains, forests, rivers, lakes, valleys, stars, sun and moon are all spiritualized; each has its own lord or master. Formerly these spirits were believed to guide and protect human beings. All the ninety-nine Tengris appear to be the personifications of the atmosphere: dull, bright, stormy, humid, hot, cold and so on.

The benevolent white Tengris look down on Earth through a door to see how humans are progressing. If any misfortunes have occurred they send down some of their children (*khats*) to help. If one looks up when the door opens glory falls on the Earth, and one becomes lucky. It is customary for Buriats to raise cairns (*oboo*) in sacred places to revere nature spirits.

The Buriat black shamans serve the underworld deities, the white shamans the heavenly divinities.

Tailagan ceremony

To escape the wrath of hostile spirits sacrifices were offered, the most widespread being the *tailagan*, a communal sacrifice honouring the clan spirits of the spiritualized places. This archaic ritual almost disappeared during the period of collectivization of agriculture after the Russian Revolution, but Tugutov was able to attend one in July 1960 in the Ulei *ulus* of the Ust-Ordin Buryat National Park, which he described in *Shamanism in Siberia* (Hoppal, pp. 267ff.)

The *tailagan* ceremony was entrusted to nine or twelve old men headed by the shaman. Each family provided cups, baskets and a sheep. The cups are consecrated by smoke from burning fir tree bark called žodo, which has the same function as the censer in the hand of an Orthodox priest.

The shaman and the old men drank *arak* or *sasali* (a kind of koumiss) out of each container and the ceremony begins with invoking the aid of the guardian spirit to whom the service is dedicated and requesting him to ensure 'Much success and good haul/Long life/lasting luck'. The spirit is told the name of the person offering the sacrifice and those who are praying to him, or more usually to a deity. Wine is sprinkled in the air for the spirit. The audience toss their bowls into the air and those that fall bottom down indicate good luck for the owner.

The second stage of the *tailagan* involved the sacrifice of a mare, killed in a most painful way by being laid on its back, legs tied up by five or six men, who then pull two legs in one direction while others pull the other legs in the opposite way. The abdominal cavity is cut open and one of the men thrusts his right hand through it, puncturing the diaphragm and breaking the aorta. The hide and hooves are hung up and the boiled flesh shared out. At a great *tailagan* four to eight mares were sacrificed. The ceremony in the Irkutsk region in 1960 was less elaborate. The sacrifice took place on a mountain before a big stone – the stone of the mountain's old man. The participants sat cross-legged in a semicircle and koumiss was placed in front of each head of a family.

Koryak spirits

Koryaks have few supreme beings, probably because of the zeal of the Russian Communists. It appears that now many former deities have coalesced into one supreme being who does not interfere much in the affairs of humans, but at death their souls go to him and hang on the posts and beams of his dwelling until it is time for them to be reborn. The length of each future life is indicated by a leather thong. Big Raven (Quikinnaqu) attends to human affairs. The Raven figures also in the mythology of the Northwest Amerindians, as well as in the myths of the Northeastern Siberians. Big Raven is transformed into a bird when he puts on a raven's coat. He appears to have been a culture hero who taught the people the use of the fire drill, how to catch sea and land animals and how to protect themselves against hostile spirits. Then he disappeared; some say that he and his family were turned into stone.

Some Koryaks believe that the owner of the sea is a woman, or that the sea itself is a woman. Evil spirits are called *kalau* (singular *kala*). Formerly, they were visible, but no longer. They are numerous and can change shape and size at will. Household utensils, parts of the house and even excrement have an existence of their own; also the cry of an animal, sounds of drums and human speech have an independent existence apart from the objects that produce them.[7]

The Reindeer Koryak fear wolves because of the danger to their herds and the supernatural powers attributed to the animal. When the wolf is in an invisible anthropomorphic shape it is most dangerous. It is said to be a rich reindeer-owner who is the powerful Master of the Tundra. He avenges himself especially on people who kill wolves. In other words the animal embodies the spirit of a powerful shaman as well as a hostile spirit.

Yekyua was one class of the three types of spirit associated with Yakut shamans that remain hidden until the snow melts, when they rise from their hiding-places and wander about. The most dangerous yekyuas are those associated with shamanesses. The weakest are those of dogs; the most powerful those of bulls, stallions, elks and black bears. The crow is a bad yekyua; eagle and hairy bull are called 'devilish fighters and warriors' – an epithet most flattering for shamans. Yekyua spirits are only visible to wizards.

Among the Ainu of Japan the supreme being is called Kotan Kara kamui, 'the maker of places and worlds, and possessor of heaven'. His other names include Tuntu, 'pillar' and 'upholder', that is, Creator.[8] There are other minor deities, some of them benevolent, but each has a malevolent double. The Wakka-ush kamui are female deities of springs, streams, lakes and waterfalls. The female who controls fish and watches over river mouths and the places where fresh and salt-water mingles is called Chiwash ekot mat. The evil god of the waters is Sarak kamui. (Sarak indicates accidental death by drowning or by some other calamity.) The Sun-goddess rules over everything that is good. There is also a Moon-god. Other deities are thought to dwell in these luminaries, hence the fear of eclipses. The Milky Way is the 'River of the Gods' where the deities fish. The Goddess of Fire resides in fire although fire itself is not worshipped. She both warms and heals the body yet she is feared because she understands the motives behind the acts and words of men. Every dwelling and all individuals have their own guardian spirits.

Samoyed deity

The Samoyed chief god is Nim or Ileumbarte (literally 'giver of life'), the ruler of Heaven and Earth, although he never visits the Earth lest he becomes polluted by it. He manifests himself in storms, rain and snow, and remains completely indifferent to the affairs of humans. If he wishes to communicate with them he does so via the spirits.

Vogul deities and Khanty and Mansi spirits

The Voguls have two classes of deities: beneficent ones (*yanykh-torum*) and malevolent (*khul*). The supreme god is the Creator, Kors-Torum, the progenitor of all other divine beings. He like the Hebrew Yahweh is invisible to human beings and never comes down to Earth. Instead he sends his eldest son Yanykh-Torum who resembles a man and whose brilliant raiment shines like gold (cf. the invisible Christian God). He never carries any weapons. Once a week he descends to Earth to see how humans are faring. If the people pray to him for rain or fair weather, he commands his younger brother, Sakhit-Torum who lives in the clouds, to do whatever is required. He drives reindeer laden with casks of water across the skies. When he whips them they leap forward, whereupon the water spills out as rain.[9] The *khul* malevolent beings can change shape, but are usually depicted as very tall with conically shaped heads. They may kill and eat humans. Another divinity, Vit-khon, lives in water and presides over fish.

Effigies of spirits are kept in forest sanctuaries by the Khantys and Mansis. Here the men periodically congregate for special rites including those for averting disease. Horses, reindeer and other animals are sacrificed and the blood smeared on the images of the spirits to 'feed them'.

Tungus cosmology postulates three worlds: the upper world of the supreme being, the middle (Earth) world and the underworld of the spirits of the dead. All these worlds are linked by a river and all of Nature is animated by occult forces and countless spirits.

Spirit conjuring is through the stimulation of our own psyche when in a receptive, trance-like state of consciousness, so that we may experience things as they are and also be more receptive to the phenomena of the shamanic world. Spirit-conjuring is cathartic, as well as hypnosis and suggestion that allows shamans and audience to experience altered states of consciousness in which other levels of existence and relationships are perceived, although without a firm belief in the world of spirits by the audience, the shaman would be unsuccessful. (Similarly, Jesus was unable to cure people who did not believe in his powers.)

Shadow spirits

The helping spirit of the Lapps is called *sveje* or shadow. There are also shadow fish, shadow reindeer and shadow snakes that accompany shamans on their journeys to the underworld to bring back dead or kidnapped souls. When a shadow animal is injured in a fight the shaman suffers the same injury – or if it is killed he too will die.[10] It is interesting that Sir Arthur Eddington, the Nobel Prize winner in physics, states that 'the shadow of my elbow resting on a shadow table, while the shadow ink flows over the shadow paper. . . . This . . .

admission that physical science is dealing with the world of shadows is one of the significant advances of recent times.'

When blue smoke appears above an East Yakut sorcerer it indicates his connection with spirits. The Vogul people speak of blue smoke that forms around a shaman which indicates the arrival of a deity. Perhaps the colour blue originated only in the eyes of the onlookers, as 'changes in magnetic fields produce electric potentials, whose effect on the eye is often described as a bright blue light. These "magnetic phosphemes" arise when an alternating current of from ten to one hundred hertz flows through a person's head.'[11] It seems that blue light emanations, shamanism and altered states of consciousness are all connected in some way.

When a spirit departs it sounds like the buzzing of a bee; when it stays it beats the drum violently, speaking its own language unless it is a wolf, fox or raven that are capable of human speech.[12] No attempt should be made to touch spirits; otherwise they will retaliate on the shaman and may kill or severely injure him or her. Spirit possession is fairly infrequent in Mongolia, but when recurrent the sufferer may become a shaman or some other occult specialist, in the hope that one's own spirit may prove more powerful than the hostile spirit.

Sometimes disease is transferred to cattle who are then sacrificed and ascend to the sky. This constitutes a sacrifice to the spirits.

Good and bad spirits

The Kamchadal's creator was made by the spirit Raven, *Kutq*. Evil spirits live in volcanoes and hot springs; spirits abound everywhere, some good and some bad. St Paul was also much occupied with the prevalence of demons and spirits which he claimed constituted the greatest hindrances that Christians have to contend with. The very air was infested with spirits. He also attributed his own infirmities to the machinations of an angel of Satan; he believed that the planetary Archontes were the demonic rulers of the world. A demonic army of 200 million is mentioned in Revelation (9. 16ff.) as well as unclean spirits in the forms of frogs and locusts. The Kamchadal people propitiate whales and walruses and venerate bears and wolves whose names are never uttered. Most clan-gods are the spirits of men who have died by drowning, by fire or been killed by bears, and sacrifices are periodically made to them.

The chief evil god of the Ainu is *Nitne kamui*. Altaian good spirits (*aru neme*) are subject to the good god Ülgen who never harms human beings. Good spirits live on seventeen levels above the Earth; the bad ones occupy nine or seven levels under it. Erlik Khan, ruler of the underworld, lives at the lowest level in almost total darkness. Originally, Erlik was a heavenly spirit. Perhaps he fell from his lofty position as did the fallen angel Lucifer. When sacrificing animals to the spirits, the victims are strangled, otherwise the sacrifice would be incomplete. The Altaian Sky Goddess, Ak D'aiyk the creating one, was sent to Earth by Ülgen to protect human beings. He sent also Chuiuk, who resembled a piebald falcon, and a grey eagle to protect Polshtop, the chief of the shamanic ancestors in the maternal line.

The fertility goddess of the Yakuts is Aisyt who dwells in the east where the sun rises. The 'white' or 'summer' shamans hold her festivals in spring or summer where she is invoked to give male progeny. The shaman sings and dances as he leads a procession of nine virgin girls and boys holding each other's hands to the celestial world where Aisyt's servants stand at the gates armed with silver whips to turn back those who are corrupt, dangerous or evil.[13]

Yakut and Enet deities

Yakuts have two great classes of gods, the celestial divinities 'above', and the subterranean ones 'below', but there is no opposition what-soever between them, as the different positions merely indicate specialization among the various religious forms and powers. Art Toyon Aga, chief of the celestial deities and spirits, dwells in the sky and is neither malevolent nor benevolent. His emblem is the sun; he speaks with the voice of thunder, but shows little interest in human affairs. Therefore, it is useless to pray to him, except in the most extraordinary circumstances. This resembles the Tungus *buga* and both are probably due to Buddhist influences as well as to the Chinese concept of the 'principle of nature' which is not an entity and is not influenced by sacrifices or prayers. There are also seven great gods above and a number of minor ones as well as the gentle mother creatrix and the 'Lady of the Earth'. Bai Baianai lives in the eastern part of the sky and in the forests. Black buffaloes are sacrificed to him showing his earthly origins. When hunting is unsuccessful, the flesh, entrails and fat of the animal are burnt by the shaman. Then a wooden figure of Baianai covered in hare skin is washed in blood.[14] The Yakut spirit of hunting (*ehekēn*) is represented by an oval calfskin-covered horn ring of irregular shape. The base of the oval resembles a human face. The spirit of hunting is locked into the ring, which is also used for divination. If it falls face up it presages good fortune and vice versa. Other *ehekēns* were fashioned from deformed willow branches in an incomplete ring with a crudely carved face. During migrations the *ehekēn* is carried on the back of a special reindeer called *tangarel*, literally 'possessor of god'.[15]

According to Yakut belief every mountain, river, lake, stone and all other movable objects have 'owner' spirits (*ichchi*). Sometimes they may be dangerous to human beings, such as the 'owner' of the wind (*kurar-ichchi*). He is a black spirit because of the damage caused by wind. When on certain journeys Yakuts use a special language so that the *ichchi* do not know what objects are referred to, as otherwise they would destroy them.

In Yakut cosmology, the east and west are places of good spirits; the north, of evil ones. The chief evil spirit is Allara-Ogonür (Underground Old Man who lives in the far north).

The Enets' 'genetrix of the earth' was *dja soj* who endowed the first couple with male and female organs. Formerly, every Enet woman possessed an image of *dja soj*. In 1962 Vasiljiev was shown a tiny parka by a young Enet woman which had the figure of the Earth's mother on it, or more precisely her body represented by a dark egg-shaped stone.[16] Another divine being is Djiri ponde, the life-giver and master of reindeer, who divided the people into nations. There are also malevolent beings, devourers of the souls of the dead, who also send diseases. In a number of Kalmuk folklore stories a grey-haired old man often appears to sleeping people. Coxwell suggests that the old man is the deity.[17] An Altaian story includes such a figure who says: 'I am God'.

It is said that a shaman's soul or spirit cannot enter a hut if a besom is laid under the threshold, for the broom is transformed into an impenetrable forest.

Important female spirit

A figure of a female spirit from a cultic place on the Kazym river was given to the Regional Museum of Khanty-Mansisk in the 1960s, together with four other figures. The female spirit appears to be the most important and consists of a round frame on a pole. On the top of the frame is a large crimson silk kerchief with tassels, over which are put silver and metal sheets placed one below the other. The whole form is reminiscent of a human head. Some pendants of fish, handbells and birds are attached. The metal sheets do not go all round the 'head' as if forming a 'face'; red threads are tied to the 'head'. Below it are scarves, marten skins and other animal hides, with twisted copper bracelets, small bells and an old metal figure of a bird. The figure is about 1.5m high. It is thought to have been made in about 500 CE. The whole thing is held together with a strip of red cloth and a plaited red leather belt.

The Khanty and Mansi people often used metal to represent the faces of spirits. Sometimes lead, copper or silver was used. The latter was fashioned from silver soup plates obtained from St Petersburg, and the silver was usually Iranian. A guardian spirit figure from a village on the Ob river was represented by a formless mass of fox skins and other hides with a small copper sheet for a face. Some spirit idols resemble wooden dolls with metal faces, stuffed bodies, but no feet.

Khanty goddess, Vut-imi

Vut-imi was the principal goddess of the Khanty groups; songs were sung about her at the bear festival and at the sacrificial fire lit near her hut. She always wore a pendant in the shape of a grey hen. In folklore the 'Great woman of the Kazym river' was called Teterej, and the holy bird of the Kazym was a grey hen. It was also a property sign, a decorative motif and a spirit that guarded sleeping children. The Grey Hen Woman cult is very ancient and 'dates from the period of matriarchal relations . . . the female spirit began to be venerated by men as well [but] women now in general had no access to the cultic places . . . [not even] to the "sacred" island of Num-to that had earlier been Vut-imi's place of residence'.[18] The spirit of the hearth fire was believed by the Evenki 'to be protectress of the clan's souls the creative (birth-giving) ancient (old) woman (mother) of the clan'.[19]

To the Nivkhi, fire was a woman. Both fire and the hearth were associated with the old woman Tkuriź who punished any violation of the hearth. The Sakhalin Nivkhi goddess of fire was Tuurm, the protectress of the clan; another clan protectress was Fadzja, the Nanai fire goddess.

Animal sacrifices

The shamans of Sakhalin Island in the far east of Siberia sacrificed animals to mountain spirits and raised cairns, dedicated to guardian spirits, along the roads. They had great respect for Nature, in common with many other unsophisticated peoples, who were among the first 'environmentalists'.

Apart from belief in the maternal origin of natural phenomena among the northern peoples, 'there existed maternal cosmogonic cults whose formation apparently can be traced back to the period in which the views of Earth as a supernatural female took shape'.[20]

Animal sacrifices in Mongolia were believed to help people by gaining the support of spirits for exorcisms or for curing purposes. It was customary to dig five holes in the direction of the five demons, and a grass figure wearing golden clothes was mounted on a horse. Later a dough figure and the bones of a horse were placed in a hole dug by the person for whom the exorcism was intended. Thus the figure becomes a receptacle for the evil influence, or a substitute for the patient's body. In cases of persistent possession among the Daurs the individuals experienced distant events or sang the songs of spirits but not in their own words. Sometimes meaningless or foreign words were used which resemble the Christian glossolalia.

Inuit society, in common with all shamanic societies, was loosely organized. All beings are regarded as essentially human in nature. In the past, human beings and animals could voluntarily change their forms, but sometime in the distant past this was no longer possible and those who were in animal form at the time remained animals and vice versa, although both humans and animals have souls. The soul resides in a vital organ such as the liver, and survives the individual's death, when it becomes a spirit. Most of the helping spirits are the souls of dead people. When an Inuit shaman's hands become covered in blood during the ritual, it is the blood of spirits.

Chukchi 'prayer paddle' and Koryak whale festival

The Chukchi Master of the Sea Keretkun's annual harvest renewal ceremony included a net with models of gulls and paddles suspended from the ceiling by a special pole that passed through the net and out through the smoke hole. The paddles had decorations painted on them in seal blood. A special 'prayer paddle' was used to convey the people's request to Keretkun for successful hunting.

For Koryaks the whale festival is an important event to honour the spirits of the whales caught and to ensure their return to the sea for future hunting. The whale spirits are offered water to drink which is placed on the household shrine among the other guardian spirits. The shrine consists of a grass mat on which are placed the anthropomorphic family guardians dressed in grass 'neckties', and a carving of a whale and a whale-shaped dish. A hood of grass is placed over the head of the whale to prevent it from seeing its body being cut up. The ceremony culminated in two women in grass masks singing incantations to the whale's spirits.[21]

Tungus spirits and animals

Tungus spirits have no physical substance but may assimilate physical phenomena into their immaterial substance. Thus the spirits may consume the essence of the sacrifice through smell, evaporation, vapour, smoke and so on, even as the Hebrew god Yahweh savoured the smell of burnt offerings. The Tungus do not believe that animals are spirits but that spirits often enter them and pass from animal to animal, or into human beings. They see a certain degree of individuality in animals. Dogs are highly regarded and are said to be mentally on a par with human beings, at least in some respects. Reindeer are more intelligent than the horse, but the cow is considered stupid. When a spirit enters an animal it may become uncontrollable or stupid, but if directed by the spirit it may become as clever as the spirit itself.

The supreme being of the Tungus is *buga* (compare the Mongol term *bogdo* (holy); Old Persian *baga*, 'god'; *bugaš* the Kassite god; and the Russian and Slavonic 'god'). *Buga* cannot be known by humans, although he regulates the life of men and animals and seems to be some kind of law of Nature. *Buga* is beyond requests or prayers which suggests some Buddhist influence.

Barguzin and Nerčinsk Tungus regard the world as having always existed which dispenses with the need for a creator. (This is also a Buddhist view.) The world is divided into three sections – upper and middle, which includes land and sea, and the lower part called *bunil* (from *buni*, the 'dead' from the stem *bu* 'to die'; the suffix l denotes the plural so the whole means 'the dead men').[22] The upper world has a number of skies where dwell a series of spirits called *burkan* or *buga*, who are brought down to Earth and placed on high mountains. Two sea snakes (*kulin*) support the land. Their movements cause earthquakes. Similarly, the mythical Hindu serpent Vasuki also supports the Earth and causes earthquakes when he moves. The entrance to the lower world of some spirits and to the souls of the dead is in the northwest area of the middle world.

Laoje is a horse-riding Tungus spirit of Chinese origin which is also beneficial to horses. In cases of illness pigs are sacrificed to *Laoje*. During the sacrifice, horses are decorated with long pieces of silk tied to their tails and manes. Then for a specific period they are not allowed to be ridden or worked. *Davai* is a spirit that protects cattle according to the nomad Tungus of Mankova and others. The Tungus sacrifice a black goat to the spirits of the underworld; a black cow takes the spirit in a southeasterly direction.

Jol is the Khingan protector of horses and cattle. His spirit resides in a special piece of leather about a foot square; on the upper part are male and female leaden images representing spirits. After the birth of colts, small bones are attached to the leather and the spirits 'fed'. An Earth spirit is Tudukan who lives under the Earth, and rides a black horse. All agricultural and equine matters are addressed to him.

Four-eyed animals are mentioned, a notion derived from observation of the skinfold under the eyes of *Cervus Elaphas* with the corresponding bone cavities formed above the eyes of the horse.[23]

Spirits are said to have taken away two of the animal's eyes, so making it possible for humans to kill deer and ride horses more easily. A 'four-eyed dog' is mentioned in the Indian horse sacrifice.

The Manchu clan spirits often leave their dwellings because of dogs' blood; hence dog meat is prohibited. Dogs are of less importance to the northern Tungus than to the Manchus, although they carry the souls of the dead to the underworld. The Reindeer Tungus of Manchuria believe they originate from a bitch impregnated by a spirit-like man of 70 years old who descended from the heavens. Similarly some aboriginal groups in China, the Ainus of Japan and other ethnic peoples share the same belief.

Spirits may be called up by whistling or hissing. Reindeer and horses are reserved for 'placing' spirits in them, or for the spirits to ride. A Tungus shaman may voluntarily introduce spirits into himself and so becomes a 'placing' for them. However, sounds of drumming and other instruments must be avoided by the uninitiated, otherwise the spirits may be attracted by the noise and enter people who would be unable to master them. Singing also attracts spirits. The shaman begins singing quietly whereupon the spirits approach him, then the singing becomes louder and more passionate, culminating in a scream of ecstasy as the spirit enters the shaman, after which the rhythm and melody changes. Some refrains are sung when the shaman goes down to the lower world to intensify the emotions and the high expectations of the audience as well as having a hypnotic effect. Such performances give deep satisfaction to the onlookers.

Werewolves

The iconoclastic Christian missionaries almost destroyed shamanism in the nineteenth century; it was even a crime to possess a drum, but some trance techniques managed to exist as well as much folklore concerning shamanic skills. The most helpful spirits were wolves. Shamans were said to be able to turn themselves into wolves and transform the dead into werewolves. The werewolf tradition is based on the belief that the dead may sometimes appear to the living, by ritual means, in the form of animals such as white ptarmigans, foxes, bears, rabbits and wolves. The mere sight of a werewolf causes mental instability. A single wolf, that is, a werewolf, is believed to be a metamorphosed shaman who had acted against his own people. Wolf packs were regarded as a group of corpses in the form of werewolves.[24]

The Enets' 'Master of the Earth' is *dja biomo*, and *ja eru* of the Nenets. He lives underground and animates the whole vegetable kingdom. The sun is worshipped by both Enets and Nenets and is regarded as female, a sign of the ancient origin of this cult. During winter the sun hides behind the horizon. When it rises, a reindeer is sacrificed and a special white reindeer with a spot on one side is dedicated to the sun and allowed to wander freely until it dies. The moon has its own Master – a shaman called Virure who once rose up to the moon, but could not return because of the powerful lunar attraction. Thus the marks on the moon are the image of Virure with his drum. Fire is also worshipped; without it nothing can live because of its great power. It has a mistress who warms it. The fire's mother was Tu ê. To the Yenisei Nenets meteorites were sacred stones which had fallen from the sky; each was guarded by a shaman. Most natural phenomena originally had feminine features, but were gradually displaced by masculine images.[25]

The customs of the north Eurasian peoples show many features of an archaic Mother-cult, especially the worship of the Mothers of Earth, Fire, Sun and Water which are preserved by the Samoyed-speaking peoples including the Nganasans, whose creatrix is Mou-jami, the most important of the Mothers. Similar beliefs concerning Mother Earth were held in the past throughout the Arctic and sub-Arctic areas as attested by the ancient incantation formulas of the Nenets, Nganasans and Yukaghirs. Mother Earth protected women in childbirth. Nganasan women wore an amulet (*simi*) on the neck, in the form of a semi-circular pouch or bag edged with a few red or gold stripes and containing various herbs, moss, fat and earth. Hot coals were also placed in it indicating the woman's connection with the sacred fire and hearth. After childbirth the woman's old amulet was left in the same place and a new one made.

The eyes of dead wild deer were dedicated to Mother Earth by placing them on the ground. Failure to do so caused various calamities. If any damage was done to the eyes a dog had to be killed, and in turn its eyes given to Mother Earth. Women were never allowed to look into the eyes of wild deer lest they give birth to monsters. Mother Earth herself gave birth to the eyes of fish which were put into the body of Mother Water to shelter them.

The cult of Mother Fire was important, for fire is a living entity that gives birth continually to girls in the form of tongues of flame. The Nganasans called Mother Fire Tu-njami, who protects the home and its inhabitants, as well as purifying individuals who have violated a sacred taboo. To Yukaghirs, Mother Fire resembled a small naked girl who protected the family and home; the Evenki regarded fire as the head of the family and of the clan; the Nivkhi saw it as a woman, Tkuriz, who punished any violations of the hearth; to Kets fire was the goddess Bokoj 'Mother Fire'; the Chukchis and Shors saw it as a woman with thirty teeth. 'Feeding' fire was a widespread custom among Russian hunters in Siberia who adopted the custom from the indigenes. Fire, sprinkled with vodka, helped the hunters in the *taiga*.

Mongolian spirits

Mongolian evil spirits (*shurkul*) are active in this world. They are nameless, ugly, red-eyed and dirty and appear only at night. They can assume the form of small animals and get into domestic objects like combs, knives or pots. Sometimes they enter people's bodies, causing them pain but not mental troubles. Far out in the steppes, they light fires in the skulls of dead animals, that burn with a bluish flame. It was safe to travel with a shaman because he had greater powers than any of the *shurkuls*.[26]

It is customary in Inner Asia to consecrate specific domestic animals to various spirits. A beloved horse that was ill could be dedicated in order to protect it, and similarly children were consecrated to Tengger. Shamanic evil spirits caused many different kinds of harm including accidents, illnesses, madness, depression, cattle epidemics, destruction of crops and livelihood.

When an animal was killed by the Mongolian Daurs to propitiate a spirit (*barkan*), the eyes were removed and 'offered separately, but only when the whereabouts of the spirit was known. The eyes were laid pointing in that direction. . . . The embodiment of directionality, the eyes "took" the animal's soul to its destination.'[27] The spirit of livestock, especially horses, was Jiyachi known to the Mongols, Buriats and various Tungus groups. It was usually represented in the form of a cloth with human shapes made of horsehair sewn on to it. Each spring it was daubed with the first food and fat of meals and consequently became evil-smelling. Tufts of calves' hair were attached to it and said to be a blessing of the calves.

Another Daur spirit is Keiden. This mysterious entity can drive human beings mad and manifests itself variously as a human being, a bird, nine human beings or thirty sky dragons. It is associated with air. The people of Eastern Asia have long associated wind with bringing disease, change and disorder as well as terrifying storms. Among the multitude of other spirits, both old and new, which are added to the cult, are Doka Barkan, the gate spirit, Auli Barkan, a mountain spirit manifested in the form of a fox, and Sum Barkan, a temple spirit who is also a fox. It was customary to keep a picture of a fox with a human head in small wooden shrines in outhouses. On New Year's Eve the fox spirit would be offered cakes, alcohol and cooked meat. Various illnesses were attributed to fox and weasel spirits which necessitated propitiation.

Womb goddess in the sky

The Mongolian moon-goddess was Ome Niang-Niang, also known as Ome Barkan. Her name or title Niang-Niang means 'mother goddess' in Chinese, and is most probably of Chinese origin with Taoist, Buddhist and Christian elements. A number of cults of the same name were widespread throughout China and Mongolia and across Inner Asia from the Altai to the Lower Amur. It involved involuntary possession and the shamanic manipulation of spirits.

Niang-Niang was concerned primarily with the procreation of children and with everything relating to their care. She was envisaged in the sky, where 'explanations' were given for human existence, life, health and disease. The Tungus spirit N'ang-N'ang was different from Niang-Niang, the former being purely a domestic spirit, all rituals taking place in the home. Many male and female spirits were associated with N'ang-N'ang, including a number of female spirits identified with various diseases and a male group associated with foxes. The cult included possession and the manipulation of spirits. There were also many ancient cults of female fertility spirits in Inner Asia, who guarded the souls of unborn children.[28]

A fearsome spirit called Bushku, one of the Niang-Niang group of spirits, seems to personify diseases including syphilis, leprosy, tuberculosis and bloody disorders. The Manchus considered it so powerful that even shamans could not control it. Offerings of menstrual or childbirth blood sometimes propitiated the spirit, at least for a time.[29]

At the dangerous time of birth the midwife prayed to Ome Niang-Niang and uttered spells, but more importantly she invoked Auli Barkan (mountain spirit) although it was really a dangerous fox spirit that lived in mountainous country. The spirit then took over the midwife and guided her through the delivery, so bringing the mother and child back into this world.

Ome Ewe ('womb mother') was an old woman who lived in a nine-storeyed pagoda, surrounded by gold and silver pine trees, with phoenix birds guarding the gate. Eggs emerged from the waters of nine hot springs, which Ome held to her long breasts by which she fed numbers of babies. Sometimes the infants played with roe-deer ankle bones inlaid with gold and silver. When the babies had grown a little, Ome would 'smack their bottoms saying: "Go" [to the human world and be born] whereupon the babies yelled "wa, wa" indicating that they were born'. The blue patch on their buttocks was the hand print of Ome. This patch 'is the "Mongolian spot", an area of dark skin genetically inherited by certain North-East Asian peoples'.[30]

The famous shamaness Huangge added an 'external' spirit called *sumu barkan* (temple spirit) to her usual spirits. Temple spirit was also an ancient fox spirit which changed from black to white over 10,000 years. It also included twelve small white animals and small deformed black creatures, which caused Huangge to hallucinate when they possessed her.

Holieri, also called *da barkan* (great spirit), dwells at the pole of the earth and paradoxically also in a number of rivers, the tributaries of the Amur. This spirit may assume various forms including a deformed hunchback with two spirits, two halves of a person struck by lightning, hairy monsters with one leg from the buttock to the sole of the foot, two golden turtles, two silver frogs, two people with no eyes, two cuckoos, two dragons, and so on.

Another spirit *olon barkan* is similar to Holieri; it too has a number of 'seats' or forms including a judge, blacksmith, merchant, fox, crow, cuckoo, deer, lizard, earthworm, dog, snake, etc.

The Teleut god Tatai is the owner of hail, thunder and rain. Tatai was an ancient Kirghiz and Buriat god. They still have the exclamation 'O Tatai!' associated with the ancient forgotten deity Tatai. A number of Tibetan Buddhist deities entered Tuva during the seventeenth century resulting in an amalgamation of Buddhist and shamanic beliefs. A shaman could even be a Buddhist priest. Tuvans are alone in believing that the gift of shamanism can be obtained from the sky through the spirit owners of the rainbow.[31]

The Evens believe that reindeer were a gift to them from the god Hövki and from the Sun-god; hence they are celestial and solar animals. The Altaic Tatars sacrifice a horse to the Sky-god, in the belief that the shaman will accompany the animal's soul to the other world.

According to Yakuts the shaman's prestige was determined by the god who had given him his chief spirit-helper, and by the height of the branch of the mythical shaman's tree on which he had been instructed by the spirits during his initiation.[32]

The above deities and spirits are but a tiny number of supernaturals belonging to the various shamanisms found in the vast area of Siberia and Eurasia.

5

The Shaman's Costume

The special costume worn when shamanizing constitutes a religious microcosm indicating a sacred presence and symbolizing the shamanic worldview. It is an independently existing object possessing its own magical power because of its in-dwelling spirits. By means of the costume the shaman is transformed into a superhuman being before the assembled people; thus the shaman becomes that which one displays. Originally, it signified the animal spirit ancestor of the shaman – the same ancestor animal of the clan. This belief lasted until the beginning of the twentieth century. It is customary to hand the costume down to the shaman's successor. An aged Ket shaman gave his regalia to his own granddaughter saying: 'Now she will shamanize for you'.

Caroline Humphrey points out that the costume is not merely a collection of indiscriminate objects, but

a construction which was a conscious appropriation of powers. It proposed its own space (the back-pad), time (the twelve year straps, the days of the year, shells), roads (the cart-track straps and the rainbow streamers), and vehicle (the drum); it incorporated the idea of the renewal (the antlers . . .) and mysterious metamorphosis-birth (the cuckoo-chick which emerged in the nest of a different species). It also established the shaman as a socio-political arena, the armed citadel . . . the shaman's plaques, arrowhead, etc. were a comment on time, since the ancient objects were fixed to a gown representing years and months.

Humphrey adds that the functions of some of the objects have been lost, and hence other meanings are given them. The costume is not a primitive thing 'unselfconsciously copied. In fact the creation of elegance, of an androgynous glamour, seems to have been a strong element.'[1]

The costume is usually a long coat hung with pieces of iron, rattles, rings and figurines of mythical animals, or pieces of material made into snake form, a breastplate, a mask, a large hat, cap or helmet, embroidered stockings and a decorative belt. All the above have mystical meanings. The shaman holds a drum or tambourine, said to have been given to him by the spirits, and by which he calls them up and collects them in the instrument which is also decorated with symbols. The meaning of some symbols is not known to non-initiates. The drum acts as his 'horse' which carries him through the air on his journeys to the celestial world.

Cloth fashioned into the shape of snakes, animals or bird skins attached to the coats of Siberian shamans are said to be receptacles for their helping spirits (*ērens*) – a tradition based on an earlier cult. Iron discs on the costume supposedly prevent the blows from hostile spirits; the discs themselves are said to have 'souls'.

A 'white' Buriat shaman has white fur and a 'black' shaman has black fur. Metallic objects representing horses and birds are sewn on the fur, and he wears a lynx-shaped cap. Some time after his initiation he receives an iron casque with two ends bent upwards to represent horns, and an iron or wooden stick-horse with a sculpted horse head on one end and decorated with bells.

A metal mirror with the figures of twelve animals is hung on the back or the front of the costumes of the Olkhonsk Buriat shamans. All these magical objects are kept in a special chest, including a large mask of leather, metal or wood, on which is painted a huge beard.

A Buriat shamaness's costume has about thirty snakes reaching from the shoulders to the ground and fashioned from black and white skin in such a way that they appear to be composed of black and white rings. One snake is divided into three at the end and is said to be essential for female shamans. She holds two staffs. Her cap is covered by a horned casque having 'antlers' projecting on both sides.[2]

Altaic shamans wear a caftan made of goat or reindeer hair with ribbons or pendants in the shape of snakes; also attached are bundles of straps of reindeer hide, as well as bells and a collar of owl feathers. The sound of the bells is the voice of the seven maidens whose symbols are sewn on the collar. A wealthy shaman should have 1,070 snakes sewn on his costume, as well as some miniature iron objects and weapons to frighten away hostile spirits; also figures of two little 'monsters' from the realm of the dead ruled by Erlik Khan. One is made of black or dark brown cloth, the other of green. The cap is decorated with swan, eagle or owl feathers.

To some tribes, including the Yurak-Samoyed, the cap is the most important part of the regalia since much shamanic power is hidden in it. In western Siberia the cap consists of a broad strip with many ribbons hanging from it. It is wound around the head and decorated with figures of lizards, and other tutelary animals.

People from the Hailar district attach knotted sacred scarves or silk streamers to their shaman dress. The more senior and successful a shaman, the greater the number of knotted scarves he receives. The knots are particularly significant since they represent the shaman's relations with the people around him. Different kinds of knots signify gifts of sheep, goats, cattle or horses; the number of knots indicates the age and sex of each animal. Some Mongolian clans called the scarves 'snakes', as did the Buriats and Tungus.[3] Real snakes were regarded as either good or bad depending on various conditions such as colour and direction of movement. Some snake figures were tied on to the costume after a performance to indicate what had happened – a black snake denoted fighting evil with evil. Some snakes remained permanently on the costume and represented the shaman's ties to the spirits.

Teleut shamans fashioned their headgear from brown owl skin, with the wings and sometimes the head attached as a form of decoration. In some regions a cap cannot be worn until after a shaman's consecration because of its dangerous supernatural qualities. During a shamanic performance the spirits will reveal when the cap may be worn without danger.

The costume endows the shaman with a new, magical body of a bird, reindeer (stag) or bear, but the most important is that of a bird and hence feathers form part of the costume, because birds have the capacity of flight. Another reason is that in some traditions the eagle is said to be the father of the first shaman and is therefore at the centre of his ecstatic flight. In some ways the eagle also represents the supreme being and denotes the sacred nature of the costume. To 'don it is to return to the mystical state revealed and established during the protracted experiences and ceremonies of the shaman's initiation'.[4]

Altaian and other shamans make their costumes resemble an owl as far as possible. The Soyot costume is usually in eagle form; the Tungus shaman's boot resembles a bird's foot, while the Yakut's displays a complete iron bird skeleton.[5]

Shaman's skeleton

Today shamanic masks are seldom worn in Siberia and north Asia, except occasionally at funerals to avoid recognition by the hostile spirits of the dead. (The original reason for Christians wearing black at funerals was to avoid being seen by demonic spirits who are attracted to corpses.) It was thought that the mask or skeleton transformed the shaman into the mythical animal ancestor, the matrix of the life of the species which dwells in the animal's bones. It is 'a matter of mystical relations between man and his prey, relations that are fundamental for hunting societies'.[6] The Samoyeds substitute a blindfold for a mask which enables them to penetrate the spirit world by their inner sight; the blindfold is also an aid to concentration. Sometimes masks represent ancestors which the wearers are believed to incarnate. Even the costume itself may have derived originally from a mask.

When a skeleton is depicted on the costume it may represent the shaman's own skeleton, or a combined bird/human skeleton. During a shamanic performance the shaman is regarded as having a half-human-half-animal nature that is, he becomes multi-faceted. The skeleton also symbolizes the death and rebirth experienced during the visions of the initiatory period, and the bones represent the whole lineage. Some ethnographers connect the bones on the costume with ancient initiation rites; others see the skeleton as a protective device, although this is a later view. Nevertheless, the skeleton concept is very old. It has been pointed out that the 'anthropomorphic "skeleton" petroglyphs of the bronze age in the Baikal region [are] figures representing shamans'.[7]

A Siberian myth relates that once shamans were killed by the spirits of their ancestors who 'cooked' their bodies, and counted the bones, fastened them together with iron and covered them with new flesh.

It has been suggested by I. R. Kortt that each member of the community is 'contained' in the garment, thereby creating a unity between the shaman and his people during the sacred ritual, but it embodies only the paternal line. However, the material surrounding the skeleton depicted on the costume may be understood as bodily flesh representing the maternal line.[8] Sometimes the skeleton is regarded as the practitioner's own body from which the shaman is spiritually reborn. The seat of the soul resides in the bones, the final source of life of both humans and animals, and therefore human beings and animals will be resurrected from them. For this reason the bones of game animals are never broken, but are carefully gathered up and buried, placed in trees or thrown into the sea. The skeleton represents the primal matter preserved by the ancestors. It re-enacts the shaman's initiation; that is, the drama of death and resurrection.

A story from South Bessarabia and North Dobrudja states that when Adam wished to provide wives for his sons, he gathered up the bones of various animals and prayed to God to animate them.[9] Resurrection from bones resembles the myth of Thor's goats of Scandinavian mythology, who came to life again after the flesh had been eaten. Another comparable myth is when Yahweh commanded Ezekiel to prophesy over a large collection of dry bones in a valley, saying: 'Oh ye dry bones, hear the word of the Lord'. Ezekiel did as he was commanded and a great noise was heard and a shaking, and the bones came together, bone to bone. They were then animated by the four winds, whereupon 'they stood up upon their feet, an exceeding great army' (see Ezekiel 37. 1–10). Bones were also preserved for resurrection in the Egyptian Book of the Dead (Chapter CXXV). Buddhists meditate on the body becoming a skeleton, thereby showing the transiency of life. Bones and skulls are important also in Tibetan Buddhism and in Tantric rites when practitioners meditate on their own bodies which reminds them that the body is composite and ephemeral and will finally disintegrate at death. Iranians put bones in 'the place of bones' (*astodan*) where they remain until the resurrection.

The Tuvan shaman's costume is called *kujak* (armour), which protects against malignant spirits. Eastern Tuva shamans have solar signs on their costumes. Solar signs are also 'found on Siberian petroglyphs, including the most ancient rock drawings in Mugur-Sargol'.[10]

Similarly, the breastplates resemble the rock drawings of the Bronze Age found in the Baikal region.

Miniature iron bows and arrows attached to the coat are intended to fight malevolent forces. Long ribbons or braids denote the ability to fly and function as wings. Boat motifs with a human being are sometimes depicted and were originally connected with the custom of catching animals in narrow defiles as they forded rivers. In northern areas these boat forms were interpreted as being spirit beings.[11]

Metal ornaments

A good shaman's garment is decorated with forty to forty-five pounds of iron; these metallic ornaments are said to resist rust and each possesses a soul (*ichchite*).[12]

A Yakut shaman's coat has an apron over it, on which are two iron circles representing breasts. His hair is dressed in a feminine style which he loosens when performing the rite. A small round disc representing the sun is attached to a leather strap hanging between his shoulders. The strap passes through the hole in the middle of the disc. Another disc of the same size and shape but with a bigger central hole represents the hole-in-ice sun and hangs below the first plate also on a strap. Thumb-sized rolls of tin hang at the back on metal rings, and tongueless copper bells are suspended below the collar on the upper part of which is an engraving of a fish's head. Flat plates about the length of a finger hang in large numbers at the back above the waist, and two round discs are tied to the shoulders like epaulets; two plates are fastened on each side and on the sleeves, and a copper plate with an engraving of a man is worn on the breast. Only a blacksmith of nine generations can make the copper breastplate without being in danger from the spirits.[13] Hollow copper balls on long straps hang like a fringe from the bottom of the coat, and a metre-long plate resembling a fish hangs from a leather strap. Some shamans have a long iron chain on the back of their coats, a sign of their great powers.

Bird and animal images

A Ket shaman wore a parka with a pointed back probably to resemble a bird's tail, and pendants in bird foot and bird form, with a headdress with bird images indicating that he impersonates a bird. Sometimes the headgear would have antlers and be linked to deer or to bears. To the Kets the Master of Animals was the bear kajyuś. Shamans could also impersonate female reindeer or the mythical bird (*gah*) or a mythical human being with bear's limbs instead of hands and feet, or the bear itself. The huge, ancient bird dag or day is portrayed among the iron objects owned by shamans; after death the bird image is kept by kinsfolk.

In Donner's Dictionary he mentions a small bell on a string called a *donde*, his 'dragonfly's tail' attached to the garment. The dragonfly often appears in shamanic songs. There are also dragonfly shamans (*duńd*). A bear shaman used a bear's paw instead of a drum when shamanizing and wore on his face a small bear's 'snout' made of skin from the animal's nose and mouth. His parka, boots and mittens were fashioned also from raw bearskin, iron pendants were in the shape of a bear's bones and he wore a tight cloth or 'bandage' around his head.

A Kandelok shaman wore elbow-length mittens made from a bear's fore paws, with boots made of the skin of the hind paws, and iron pendants representing bear's paws. Bears assisted these shamans and also supernatural earth beings, especially the *alel* family patronesses depicted as female figures and images of the dead.

Nganasan shamans had more than one costume, as specific costumes were required for specific rites. A deerskin costume helps a shaman communicate with the upper world. A stripe, five centimetres wide and ornamented with red and black triangles, was sewn around the garment using the hair of a wild deer. The right side of the garment representing the sun, the day and spring is painted red the left side is black, denoting the moon, darkness and winter. Below the waist are depicted two bears, the shaman's helpers. They pull a sledge, one runner of which indicates winter, the other summer. So fast do the bears travel that they are invisible to human beings but their presence is felt by a strong whistling wind. Bears protect against all lies and evil.[14] Near the top of the costume are four leather bands holding two quadrangular copper sheets with two knobs on each, and four raised dots forming a diagonal cross. The knobs resemble a human face and depict the life-giving spirit called Niluleminuo. On the right-hand (red) half of the costume is a round, open-worked, copper pendant on a leather band with notches in the form of two five-pointed stars. Near the shoulder-blades is a copper plate representing a bear's paw with five claws and raised dots denoting veins and bones. Just below are two small, crescent-shaped pendants fastened on straps and a hand bell so essential when shamanizing in the lower world, otherwise the shaman could not return to earth.[15] Mittens are attached to the sleeve ends and painted red. The breast cover, sixty-one centimetres long, is worn on the naked body and is made of the same skin as the garment. The hair side is worn facing inwards and sewn round with fur with red fringes at the bottom. Drawings and ornaments are stitched with the dewlap hair of wild deer, and bordered with black and red triangles. In the centre is a circle representing the shaman's navel. An iron mask at the top is an image of the spirit Moredjali (literally 'earthly day', 'daylight'), the Master of the lives of people, deer, birds and plants. His nine maidservants are represented on the lower part of the breast cover by a copper sheet with nine 'cogs' each having eyes marked by hollow sockets, and a bulge denoting the nose, but with the mouths omitted.

A shaman's fur boots are seventy-five centimetres long and are similar to those worn by ordinary Nganasans. The outer hide is painted red with black designs. A little above the instep is a black stripe, with three vertical stripes to the right and left representing the 'legskins of deer'.

The Nganasans who have both male and female shamans live in a remote part of the northern Asian territories of Russia, and so have managed to preserve much of their ancient culture up to recent times. The black triangles on the back of the coat 'signified the spinal column and "fortified" the shaman's own backbone'.[16] The iron pendants are kept in the family after the shaman's death. Small iron sheets are supposed to break the ice when the shaman descends into the frozen underworld. Pieces of bent wire represent the heads of six geese which assist him to fly to the gods. The breast cover is a trapezium, its sides made from the clipped hide of wild deer edged with black triangles, and cords holding bundles of wolf and fox hair. Copper chains are used to seize souls from the lower world. When captured, the shaman secures them to the 'three tails' of his costume. His headband has red and blue fringes hanging down before his face; the coat is stitched with the dewlap hair of a wild deer said to bring success in hunting. Underground there is water into which the souls dive, closely followed by geese and loons, so the shaman has goose wings decorating his costume. The shaman Kheripte stated that the 'goose was god at birth'. (This bird is also important in Hinduism. It represents the pure soul and the highest spirituality.) Although the shaman becomes a special being through his visionary initiation, he still requires his helping spirits who otherwise would run aimlessly about. In other words the costume is a focus for the spirits.

An important amulet of Nganasan shamans was the so-called 'shaitan's hand' (*kojka djutju*), cut from a piece of sheet iron and worn on the wrist. Beads hung from it, together with small copper wheels taken from watches.

A Tuva shamaness

The grave of the Tuva shamaness Matpa Ondar who died in 1958 shows Tibetan Buddhist influences. Her grave is not marked. About twenty metres uphill lay a bronze mirror, the lid of a Buddhist prayer shrine wrapped in blue silk and a small bundle of Tibetan Buddhist prayers. At some distance from the grave the rest of her insignia were hidden in a cave with the entrance blocked by stones. Her drum, drumstick and headdress were wrapped in her gown and lay on a white cloth on the ground. Her round drum has a carved image of herself. Her headdress consists of a small conical cap trimmed with orange-coloured cloth with two red fringes in front between which is a brocaded ribbon. The ribbon has a rhomboid design in black and orange threads. Strings of beads and maral teeth on woollen yarn hang from the edge of her cap, the front of which has a 'mask' with the eyes marked with cornelian beads. On top are some hollow copper pipes with eagle feathers tucked into them. Her goatskin costume has sleeves which are tighter towards the wrist. On the hem are two rows of fringes of dressed skin. On the upper right shoulder-blade a leather loop holds a metal ring from which hang fifty-nine snake plaits, each sixty centimetres long – other snake plaits are made of twisted woollen threads. At the upper ends of the plaits are small corals or beads for eyes. On the left shoulder-blade is a bunch of fifty-seven 'snakes'. The girdle resembles a red snake plait sewn on to the waistline. More snakes are depicted on the richly ornamented sleeves.

Her drum of western Tuvan style has a crossbar with seven pendants hanging from it, the longest pendants resembling snakes, her helping spirits. Snakes also symbolize 'armour'; that is, protection. Her snakes are partly red, white and black indicating that she had good, neutral and hostile spirits as helpers. Snakes were also believed to help in expelling disease (see the caduceus of Western medicine).

Matpa Ondar's costume also has tri-coloured tobacco pouches some of which contained remnants of tobacco. Altaian shamans' costumes also had tobacco pouches which are said to 'be a means of inspiration for them during the act of shamanizing'.[17] Ondar's costume is now in the Museum of Anthropology and Ethnology of the Academy of Sciences of the USSR.

Of the two main types of costume of the northern Tungus and those of Trans-Baikal, one is duck-shaped, the other reindeer-shaped. Metre-long broad ribbons called snakes (kulin) hang from the back. They assist the shaman in his journeys to the underworld; the concept of the 'snakes' was borrowed from the Buriats and from the Turks; the 'horses' from the Buriats.[18] The boots resemble a bird's foot.

Headgear

There are a number of resemblances between the Tibetan Bon oracle-priest's costume and that of the shaman. Both include eagle feathers, broad silk ribbons, a shield, a lance and so on.[19]

The headgear is important, for it contains a great deal of the shaman's power. It also closes up the hole at the top of the head through which the soul may escape. Donner has pointed out the importance of the cap in the ancient rock paintings and drawings of the Bronze Age.[20] In western Siberia the cap resembles a turban with ribbons, and figures of tutelary animals. Other shamans' headgear has iron antlers attached. The tines on a Solon shaman's cap increase as he conquers more and more hostile forces. The new points appear at the time when grass grows on the steppe. The headgear of a Mongolian

Daur shaman had five multicoloured scarves attached to the antlers. They represent the rainbow, the road taken by the shaman on his journeys. A fringe covers the front of the cap with a glass mirror from which light glitters to terrify demons. Between the antlers is the form of a cuckoo, the shape taken by the shaman's soul and the first bird he summons after initiation. Male and female cuckoos are also placed on the shoulders of the costume and act as messengers. It has been pointed out that the combination of antler and bird-headed tines is very ancient, first appearing in south Siberia, Mongolia and the Ordos in about the fifth century BCE.[21]

The Samoyeds of the north and the Altaians of the south have hats decorated with feathers; those of some Teleut shamans are made from brown owl skin complete with wings and head. Such ornamentation gives the shaman a new magical body in bird form. Other clans have eagles, owls and other birds depicted on their costume.

The tassels and fringes on a Chukchi shaman's cap were used for magical purposes and consisted of alternating pieces of black and white fur, as well as a small knife, the handle decorated with magical objects and a small flat piece of ivory. Highly effective amulets are fashioned from round pieces of skin with a tassel in the centre and are much favoured by the Chukchi, Koryak and Asian Inuits (the ancient Hebrews believed that tassels and fringes averted the attacks of demons).

The high hat worn by Nanai shamans is sometimes supported by a frame from which hangs long strips of animal fur with metal plaques, rings, bells and other objects. Two or four metal plates are also attached and resemble moose antlers, but an old Nanai shaman denied that they were antlers. It has been suggested that the headdress symbolized the 'relationship between the shaman and his ancestor spirit'.[22]

Some Nanai shamans see the antler-like shapes as the roots of the World Tree. Manchurian shamans' hats are crowned with the Cosmic Tree and a bird.

A Yukaghir and Chulym shaman

A Yukaghir shaman draws on the power vested in the ancestral shamans depicted on the left side of his costume; on the right side are bird skins that enable him to achieve his ecstatic flight to the upper world.

The Chulym Turks dress their shaman before the ritual. A ring is put on his finger, a cloth tied round his head, and a necklace of white beads. The necklace has the same number of beads as his rattle has rings. Every two years a bead is added to the necklace and a ring to the rattle, denoting the number of times he has ascended to the heavens. It has been suggested that the rings symbolize the 'different heavenly spheres that the shaman visited during his exercises'.[23] After a shaman's death the symbolic decorations and miniature weapons on the costume could have dire effects if not controlled and cared for by the next generation, for these weapons constantly interact with dangerous invisible powers which they have been designed to confront.[24]

6

Divination and Healing

Divination

Shamanic divination is based partly on a knowledge of natural lore, and partly on an understanding of group psychology.

In the circumpolar region, divination is usually monopolized by shamans but not entirely. Sometimes it is done by interpreting the cracks in the burnt shoulder bone of a ram or a sheep. (An animal's bone symbolizes the mystery of life and regeneration.) This method is used especially by Kalmyks, Kirghiz and Mongols; a seal's shoulderblade is used among the Koryak. The same method was employed in ancient China from the Shang period and has also been used in other parts of Asia since prehistoric times.[1]

Some shamans divine by the bow into which the spirits collect; from the quivering of the bow and its sound as it is bent with greater or lesser force by the diviner as he holds it close to his ear. Another method is by looking into fire along the bow's string. Sometimes the shaman holds a small bow in the right hand, with his thumb and forefinger holding the middle of the string, thereby balancing the bow. Then he waits for it to move on the string as on an axis, so that he can answer the questions of enquirers. The invisible power of the spirit that the shaman is questioning moves the bow.

The birchwood drumstick (qallaq) of the Chulym Turks was shaped like a shallow spoon and used for divination as well as other purposes. To learn the outcome of a person's illness, the spoon was thrown on the ground. If it fell bottom-up three consecutive times, this indicated that the patient would recover. The drumstick was also regarded as a 'whip' used by the shaman to urge on his horse on his way to the underworld.[2]

Divining bones were used by the Yakuts: either forty-one bones of turbot, or the same number of pieces from the hooves of a sacred deer. A question was whispered to one of the pieces, and a bone waved over the head three times. Then the bones were arranged in three heaps on a table, from which three pieces at a time were taken from each heap until less than four bones were left on each heap. The remainder was arranged roughly as a human figure, and each bone indicated the best direction for hunting. Then they were thrown out and their positions determined the fate of man, successful hunting, finding lost animals and so on. Another method is to heat a deer's shoulder-blade smeared with fat and then observe the way it breaks when extra heat is applied. After use it is hung on a tree, or placed on a platform. Seal shoulder-blades are used among the Reindeer Chukchi and the Evenks; the coastal groups divined with whale shoulder-blades in the whale ceremony. In each case a shoulder-blade was heated and the cracks interpreted – most questions related to the location of whales and the paths their spirits took in returning to the sea after the ceremonies.

Another divinatory method was to suspend a stone, wooden amulet or animal skull, which would swing when the correct answer was given. Ravens indicated the direction of fleeing animals to Siberian hunters. For this service the bowels and intestines of the slaughtered animals were given to the birds. The Tungus-speaking people never kill an animal for sport, but only when needed; wounded animals were always followed and killed.[3]

Healing

Magical healing is one of the main functions of Central and North Asian shamans. Various views are held concerning the origin of disease: the patient's soul may have been stolen by a spirit or it has strayed; a magical object (or objects) has entered the patient's body; or the sufferer is possessed by hostile spirits. Soul loss appears to be connected with partial loss of consciousness, as in coma, fever or delirium. Intruding spirits cause physical injury and ailments, but no loss of consciousness. The shaman summons his helping spirits to assist him in removing the intruding object – animate or inanimate – by sucking movements, sweeping with feathers and so on. Illness is regarded as an alienation of the soul.

The intruding spirits must be either placated or driven out, or taken into the shaman himself who learns the type of sacrifice into which the spirits can be sent. But wherever the patient's soul has gone the shaman pursues it, even down to the realms of the dead, the dwelling place of Erlik. To gain its release involves costly sacrifices, and a surrogate must be found and caught by the shaman who then takes it to Erlik, whereupon the surrogate soul's owner will die, but the patient will die three, seven or nine years later.

Some shamans, when coming out of their trance, have the intruding spirits supposedly in their hands which they return to the patient through the ear or the mouth. (A similar notion is reflected in the story of the Spirit of God entering the Virgin Mary's ear.) An Uzbek shaman's spirits show him the diseased parts of the patient, which appear black.

To recover spiritual health necessitates restoring the balance of the spiritual forces, because sometimes the disease is caused by neglecting the infernal powers. A number of healing methods are used including those based on logic, hypnosis, intuition, telepathy, autosuggestion, the interpretation of dreams and a kind of psychotherapy by encouraging the patient and giving hope of recovery.

A person may have three or seven souls. According to Chukchi and Yukaghir belief, at death one soul remains in the grave, one descends to the lower world of shades and one ascends to the celestial world. Other clans believe that one soul disappears at death, or is eaten by demons. Of the three souls of the Buriats, one dwells in the bones and one in the blood, which can leave the body in the form of a wasp or a bee; the last soul resembles a ghost.

Tatar, Buriat and Mongolian shamans practise the ritual of 'calling back the soul'. If it fails to return the shaman searches for it. A Buriat shaman seats himself by the patient, surrounded by a number of objects, including an arrow from which a red silk thread is attached to a birch tree erected outside the *yurt*. The thread enables the soul to re-enter the patient's body and therefore the entrance to the yurt is left open. Near the tree a horse is tethered. It will be the first to perceive the return of the soul, whereupon it will shiver. Formerly in England shivering was regarded as a bad omen indicating that either a spirit was near or death itself. In Brittany an unexplained shiver is said to be the touch of Ankou, the Churchyard Watcher – a certain death omen.

Another curative method is used when the shaman drums near the patient, massages his body and stupefies him with smoke from a specific wood and from incense. Hypnosis and suggestion are also used. Some shamanic methods are very effective but are not understood by modern medicine, 'because European medicine itself is an ethnographical phenomenon'.[4] The Yakuts believe their first ancestor, Elliei, was also the first smith. Unlike shamans, smiths can heal by natural means without the help of spirits.

The shaman healer and diviner uses methods that are partly cunning and partly practical psychology. (Most, if not all, of Jesus's cures were of psychosomatic maladies.)

A healing session of the Chulym Turks was always held late at night, in a room fumigated with burning Chinese fabric in a copper scoop. The shaman sat on a stool; earlier he had sat on a wrought iron or copper chest, in which the malevolent spirit had hidden the soul of the patient and from where the shaman had to remove it.[5] The spirits of diseases often appear in the form of dogs.

Formerly, the Nenets (Siberian) shamans believed that sickness was caused by a specific spirit which blew into the patient's mouth whereupon the shaman appealed to Num, the chief celestial spirit, to compel the hostile entity to leave the patient. Then the patient left the tent and Num caused the wind to blow away all traces of the disease. Illness could also be caused by worms. In this case they were removed by the spirit making an incision, but if the ailment had been sent by Num the shaman refused to shamanize. He knew this because the spirits told him. Another indication was if the sacrificed deer went into convulsions – a sign that the patient would recover.

Nenets shamans of the second category were healers, finders of lost deer and shamanized only at night. The method used to find the deer was to strike a wooden cup or tree stump with an iron axe which 'stuck' firmly when the spirit spoke, after which it could be removed easily.[6]

The third category of shamans indicated where the dead should be buried, and then they saw the deceased's soul off to the next world. All accounts of people cured of serious illness show the same pattern and motifs that characterize the shaman's journey into the beyond. This most elemental experience is the core of many religions and of all tribal religions.[7]

Occasionally a Mongolian shaman would agree to perform a *dolbor*, the night journey undertaken to fetch a soul from the other world, when a patient was dangerously ill. The way went through dark realms where the shaman's own life was threatened. The ritual was performed with set episodes, after which magical actions were performed to remove the spirits attacking the patient. In other exorcisms the shaman rubbed his drum on his chest and heart-mirror, so empowering the air which he blew over the patient; he also blew sacred water from his mouth and stroked the patient's body with his mirror. The sudden coldness may have had a curative effect, as formerly the cold water of holy wells in the United Kingdom was said to have effected some cures. In the above context, the attacking spirit entered the mirror and then was transferred to a human-shaped stone image called *beemee*. Fresh blood from a sacrificed chicken was put on the mouth of the image which was then burned.[8]

When shamanizing over a sick woman seven cups of barley or meal beer are offered to the chief underworld spirit. Nine cups of beer are offered for a man. The beer ransoms the victim's soul. The shamaness Shimit-kyrgys, when shamanizing over a patient made ill by the 'meddling of spirits' of water or earth, imitated the cries of raven, crow, wolf, stag, marmot and bear, but if the illness was caused by the anger of domestic animals, she imitated the sounds made by a nanny-goat, sheep, camel, horse and dog.

Shamanic healing methods have never been properly studied in the West, and are usually dismissed as 'faith healing'. Western medicine reduces illness only to the focal point of the disease – holistic medicine is seldom practised – because Western culture favours accumulation, analysis and storing up, whereas the shaman favours emptiness, from which he draws out fresh knowledge and energy. This resembles the Mahayana Buddhist concept of *śūnya*, 'void' (of permanence) or 'nothingness'. But the existence of the empirical world is not denied but only declared void of ultimate reality when stripped of its artificially conceived attributes. *Śūnya* cannot be made fuller or be decreased. It is a plenum in the philological Latin sense, not in the philosophical sense.[9]

Shamans draw their knowledge and healing techniques from the realm of transformative experience. It is interesting that recent micro-physical research shows that energy – that is, also matter – is apparently generated out of nothingness resulting in the formation of the material world.[10] The Ainu shamaness Husko told the Japanese researcher Ohnuki-Tierney that it is impossible to grasp real knowledge in words – the only way to learn something of shamanism is to become a shaman oneself.[11]

When a sick man was treated by the Yukaghir shaman Karaka-Polut (the name means 'old Koryak'), the shaman's egg-shaped drum was brought to the site before he arrived. After a number of preliminaries including throwing fat and food on to the fire, the shaman donned his fringed and embroidered cap in which most of his power is concentrated, and sat on the floor. He whistled, struck the drum and imitated the cries of various birds and animals. Then he sang: 'Mother Fire, be strong with thy heat! Mother of the dwelling, do not in thy strength endure evil!'

If the disease has been caused by a local devil the shaman says: 'Thou art our mother! Favour me and depart to thine own land!' Then he turns to the door saying: 'My protectors approach!' and drawing in deep and noisy breaths he sucks in his helping spirits. A spirit asks why it has been summoned and the shaman replies that an invisible being from below has come to torment the patient, whereupon the spirit asks for good incense and for the Russian weed that stupefies. The assistant places incense on the fire beside the shaman who inhales it through wide open mouth. More incense is thrown on the fire by the assistant who offers the shaman a pipe which he smokes for a while. Then he goes to the patient and endeavours to bite off the infected part and so draw out the disease-causing spirit which fights back furiously, but the shaman's own spirits overcome the invading spirit, whereupon he falls back exhausted into the arms of his assistant, shakes violently, has convulsions and finally sits down on the floor. The hostile spirit speaks through him and requests the five-rouble colourless water (vodka) and a black fox with a white breast, after which he will leave the patient. The shaman stands up, blows on the patient and strokes him and strikes his drum gently saying: 'Close the devil's road, so that he shall not return; act vigorously!' Then he sits down facing the door still drumming gently. With his left hand he throws his mallet back over his head, removes his cap with his right hand and throws it backwards. He pretends to remove his right eye and throws it on the floor, saying: 'Keep watch below!' He removes his left eye and throws it upwards, saying: 'Keep watch above!' He imitates the cry of the Arctic duck, takes a spoonful of water, spits it out and so ends the ceremony.[12]

For successful healing in any culture, emotion must be aroused, but there is no need for a deity to do the healing, since any method that 'induces great "excitement" leading to a suitable degree of exhaustion [as in ecstatic healing] and consequent alteration in brain function can work miracles on its own'.[13] Faith healing and spirit possession rarely, if ever, occur in a calm rational atmosphere, because emotion can be induced more easily by loud rhythmic music and dancing. In the West similar effects may be achieved by hell-fire preaching, pop music and drugs.

Yakuts, Dolgans and Tuvans only consecrated certain domestic animals – a rite performed by shamans. It was forbidden to kill a consecrated animal, and only the owner was allowed to ride it. Disease could be transferred to an animal, but if no animal was available it could be transferred to a wooden image.

The Enets and Nenets believe that smallpox and measles appear to people in human shape. In 1974 the aged Nivkhi shamaness Kazyk shamanized over a sick member of M. Taksāmi's expedition. She said she felt strong and well when shamanizing as her spirits enjoyed the 'activity'.

Dolgan Sajtāns

The Dolgan peoples use man-made or natural objects called *sajtāns* (the Arabic word for an evil spirit which is also in use among some Siberian clans). When healing a person a shaman trampled on a small stone which will be the sick person's *sajtān*. If the patient finds and keeps the stone he will recover. Shamans also uttered incantations over stones pulled up in fishing nets, smearing them with blood and keeping them in special bags made of salmon trout skins. Large boulders and rocks could also become *sajtāns*, especially those which resembled human figures.

Formerly, trees were regarded as *sajtāns*, which protected people from disease. During a smallpox epidemic a Dolgan shaman instructed the people to go through a hole in a specific tree to be cured. This is reminiscent of the curative holed stones of Cornwall which were used for the same purpose. The iron pendants representing birds and animals of the upper world decorate a dead shaman's costume and function as his guardian *sajtāns*.

Towards the end of the nineteenth century, a Yakut healing ceremony held in a hide tent was attended by Waclaw Sieroszewski. The men sit along the right side and the women on the left. The host places a pliant loop of twigs around the shaman's neck and passes the end to one of the audience, lest the spirits should seize the shaman and carry him off. Everyone relaxes and food is eaten. The shaman, on his platform of honour, unwinds his plaited hair, muttering and giving instructions while gazing fixedly at the fire. When the fire dies down, he takes off his tunic and puts on his ritual costume, then smokes for a long time while coughing and shaking. He lies on a white mare's skin and drinks cold water. Cries of birds are heard and the clanging of iron. Then after a complex ceremony the shaman chants: 'Strong bull of the earth, horse of the steppes, I, the strong bull, bellow!, I, the horse of the steppes, neigh!'

The Tungusan-speaking peoples do not believe that all diseases are caused by spirits but usually only those of delirium and insanity. The Tungus Evens of north-east Siberia use the velvet from young reindeer horns as a tonic. The velvet is singed and eaten and the blood from inside the antlers is drunk. Other tonics are *oir* fern and ginseng infusions which are taken every three, twelve or forty days. Poplar (*sul*) buds are used as painkillers. For liver and stomach complaints, rheumatism, abscesses, ulcers and dysentry, bear's gall is used.[14] Seriously ill relatives were treated by a specially chosen reindeer to be the patient's protector and known as *kud'ai*. It had to have a divine mark, be white or piebald and have a *tigok*, a ball of hair sometimes found on a deer's neck. A rope was made from the hair for the ritual gate to the celestial world composed of two young larches. The *kud'ai* brings happiness to both men and animal and can even save its owner from death, as the illness is transferred to the animal. After fumigating both patient and deer the patient spits thrice on the animal's muzzle, so passing the disease to the animal in the saliva. Henceforth the deer is allowed to run free until its death.

When a disease spirit from the lower world attacks a patient, the shaman ritually transfers it into a pair of red wooden birds in the shapes of loons or hawks, attached to two sticks, and makes them fly away with the disease and so the patient recovers. Once the disease spirit is divided into two it becomes so weakened it cannot return. The reindeer was sent to the Evens by the supreme god Hövki and the Sun-god, and hence they are regarded as celestial and solar animals. However, these animals suffer greatly from pneumonia in summer when the daytime heat changes into extreme cold at night. To effect a cure the shaman parts the hair on the deer's withers and spits into it three times. The Evens believe that evil spirits come up from the underworld to the Earth's surface through swamps and ravines; dead trees also impart an earth energy detrimental to humans.

A shamaness who fell ill in 1970 asked a woman to heat some iron until it was red hot and then to give it to her. She licked the iron continuously until it cooled and said it had calmed her soul at last, whereupon she slept until the next morning when she awoke completely cured.

Curative animals

In folklore, the shaman's reindeer are white and spotted, and are capable of averting hostile spirits and exerting a purifying force. This purity was contained in the dewlap hair and in the hair at the base of the tail. A reindeer was led to a sick person and healed the patient 'by a whiff of the sacred animal's breath'.[15] This is reminiscent of the Parsee custom of bringing a dog into a sick or dying person's room.

The cure of some serious illnesses necessitated the dedication or sacrifice of a horse, a ram or a cow to the Master mountain spirits called, in Tuva, *tailyan*. Another healing method was to sacrifice a horse on a platform erected in the mountains. The shaman drew three ochre-coloured lines on the hide, so forming the six-pointed 'crux' symbolizing the animal. Its mouth was stuffed with grass, and the head and hide were propped up on a pole. Sometimes several horses were sacrificed but all had to be of the same colour. At other times the shaman dedicated a live horse to the Master Spirit and the animal was brought to the sick man's tent by his son, who pushed the horse's head through the entrance enabling the patient to touch it. Then the horse was urged to take upon itself the evil spirits possessing the patient, or to expel them in some other way. Coloured ribbons were tied to the bit, mane and tail, after which the bit was removed and the horse allowed to rejoin the herd. Grey horses were consecrated to the god of the upper world, red and white horses to the Master mountain spirits.[16]

Evenk healing rite

A. F. Anisimov described an Evenk healing rite held in 1931. A small fire burned in the middle of the semi-dark tent, with the audience sitting around the sides of the tent. The Shaman faced the entrance. His nervous face was pale as he gently swayed to and fro. To his right and left were the images of the spirits – the salmon trout, two pole knives, fish spears and a splintered larchwood pole. More spirit images of salmon trout surrounded the fire. The assistant dressed the shaman in his ritual clothes, including a cap surmounted by an iron 'crown' with reindeer horns. The shaman sat on a raised platform representing the spirits of fish and began to drum. Then in a melodious voice he sang to evoke the spirits. Such invocatory songs are always rhymed and very beautiful. After each verse the audience joined in the chorus, after which the shaman addressed each of the spirits in turn, describing their forms and supernatural powers. As soon as the song finished the voices of the spirits could be heard as bird calls, the whirring of wings or the snorting of beasts, according to which spirit was appearing at the time. Then by yawning the shaman received the spirits into himself and gave them their orders. His animal double and the other spirits went down to the lower world by means of the World Tree to find the cause of the clansman's illness from the shaman's ancestor-spirit. But if the ancestor-spirit failed to discover the cause the animal double was sent to the upper world to the supreme being.

The shaman's songs described the animal double to the other world, accompanied by frighteningly wild gestures, screams and snorts. Screaming his last words to the spirits, the shaman became more and more entranced. Then throwing the drum to his assistant, he seized the thongs of the tent poles and began a frenzied dance accompanied by his assistant's persistent drumming, and the eerie noises of the spirits. His ecstatic state influenced those present, some of whom fell

into states of mystical hallucination, feeling themselves as if partici-
pating in the ritual or possessed by spirits. Finally the shaman fell on
to the rug foaming at the mouth, and lying as if dead. His assistant,
fearing that he would be unable to return to the middle world, begged
him to return quickly from the lower world, whereupon the shaman
stirred and a faint babble of the spirits was heard, signifying that the
animal double and accompanying spirits were returning while
the assistant beat the drum louder and louder. The shaman danced
again but in a peaceful manner, symbolizing the return of the spirits.
He told the clansman the advice the ancestor spirits had given his
animal double concerning the best way to combat the disease spirits.
Then he was offered pipe after pipe of tobacco which he smoked
avidly. (The North American Indians use tobacco as a drug.)

Before a shaman can heal, he must heal himself. Only then can he
act in sympathy with Nature's laws. 'He does not cure symptoms, but
the "idea" of the sickness'.[17] Unlike doctors the shaman does not act
in his own name, but in the name of the spirits that heal.

7

Soul, Ancestor Cults and Death

Soul

Soul dualism is found in many parts of the world, including America, parts of Southern Asia, Old Europe, Africa and among a number of circumpolar tribes and nations. This dualism originates in the old hunting cultures which formerly covered enormous areas. But later, in Europe, the concept was overlaid by Christian monistic beliefs, although some vestiges of the idea live on in folklore. Nevertheless, it remains a central part of shamanism.[1] Only shamans are able to see souls.

The shaman has a body soul that sustains his life as well as a free soul that goes in search of the lost souls of other people. In states of dream, coma and trance, a soul can distance itself from the body.

A suicide's soul can never enter the realm of the dead, being destined to wander forever on Earth. (In Christianity suicides were not allowed to be buried in consecrated ground.) The souls of women who die violently wander the Earth until the time they should have died but for the violence. Two malicious spirits emanate from human souls in the form of an evilly disposed bird (*mu-shubu*).[2]

According to Daur belief the loss of soul does not imply physical death but a state of psychological numbness. This usually occurs in babies or young children. The slightest fright can cause a baby to lose its soul. If by performing various magical acts the child's soul cannot be found, a shaman is called in, who will call back the soul and place it in the child under the protection of the Womb-Spirit (Ome Barkan). When describing a child's consecration to Ome, bright cloths, toys and some of the child's hair are wrapped in red and yellow cloths and put into a bag which is then tied up. It is very important for sacred things to be enclosed. The soul was called into the bag and then it and a bronze mirror were attached to a picture of the Womb Spirit. The shaman called out any diseased demons in the child and danced around him or her while gently beating his drum and singing a kind of lullaby. Adults, having stronger energies than children, are able to keep their souls firmly attached to their bodies. It was rare for the souls of adults to be stolen.[3] The soul of an animal or adult can leave the body when dreaming; a sigh during sleep indicated that the soul was leaving the body from the mouth, which leaves the body vulnerable to the ingress of spirits, although the soul could meet the ancestors in the realm of the dead. Shamans are able to dream specific dreams that will reveal the truth.

The Oroch believe that the soul passes from world to world while changing its shape, becoming smaller at each stage until it reaches the moon, from where it falls back to Earth to be reincarnated.[4] According to the Tuvans a man becomes a shaman when a dead shaman's soul lodges in him. This occurs at a time when black clouds appear and then a rainbow, one end of which strikes the man who forthwith becomes a shaman.

Three souls

Most Turko-Tatar and Siberian peoples are believed to have three souls, one of which remains always in the grave after death. Buriats too believe in the existence of three souls; the lowest resides in the lowest part of the human body and in the skeleton, which is the visual frame of the shamanic costume, outlined on the boots and cloak.[5] The lowest soul is an invisible copy of the skeleton, and if a bone is broken the soul is harmed. Animals, in common with human beings, also have souls, a view also held in the Old Testament: 'For that which befalleth the sons of men befalleth beasts; as the one dieth, so dieth the other; yea, they have all one breath; so that a man hath no preeminence above a beast' (Ecclesiastes 3. 19f.).

When an animal is sacrificed the bones are always protected from injury, otherwise the soul would be injured and the sacrifice rejected by the deity.

The second soul in its original state is anthropomorphic and lives in the trunk of the human being, in the heart, liver, lungs, larynx and blood. This soul is easily frightened and flees from danger, often leaving the body which necessitates tempting it back to its owner. The third and highest soul is the one that in its passing marks the end of life for the individual. This soul has the good or bad character of its owner; if good it will be requested to intercede on behalf of the clansmen, if evil it will be the cause of sickness in children and in women; therefore it has to be propitiated.

The Tungus also have a threefold soul, though this was not originally a Tungus concept. It was one of the modifications of vulgarized Buddhist concepts adopted by the Manchus from the Chinese and Central Asian groups.

Of the three souls of the Tungus the most important is the second soul. If lost it is impossible for the individual to survive. After death, it leaves the corpse on the seventh day. Sacred ashes are placed on the threshold to discover the kind of footprints left by the soul which may be those of a man, horse, reindeer, chicken or other animal. The third soul remains with the corpse for a time and then dwells with the deceased person's family. A number of people have seen their dead parents in dreams, visions and hallucinations. Wolves and foxes know when the soul leaves the body and they begin to bark. Animal and human souls are unstable and may disintegrate, but without completely killing the living organism.[6]

After death an individual's good and bad deeds are weighed which determines the kind of future life he or she will have in the next world. (The weighing of souls was common in ancient Egypt.) It was also believed that the effects of good and bad deeds determine a person's future which may indicate Buddhist influences.

Forest trees in the region of the Ket river have dolls placed in them which represent souls. Plants also have souls; other souls belong to various parts of the body – nose soul, limb soul and so on (the Hebrews of the Old Testament had the same notion). A soul often assumes beetle form and hums like a bee when in flight. When the cry of a raven is heard at night it indicates that a person's soul is leaving the body.

The Koryak word for soul is *uyicit*, which implies some vital principle in it such as 'breathing'; another term is *wuyil-wuyil* which means 'shadow'. To the Tungus 'life' is termed *èrga* which means 'to breathe'. In the Old Testament man is said to have become a 'living being' (*nephesh*); the equivalent Babylonian term *napishtu* also means 'life'. Thus the soul in pre-exilic times is not something added to a body, but in post-exilic times body and soul were regarded as essentially different components making up a human being. During the Hebrew festival of the Great Pardon, the High Priest was required to remain awake the whole night lest his soul left his body and would then be unable to return. Thus a passage in the Song of Songs reads: 'My soul failed when he spoke'. The Hebrew term, rendered in English as 'failed', really means 'went out', thereby indicating that the soul leaves the body in sleep, trance, ecstasy or during extreme excitement. The ancient Mesopotamians called a sorceress 'a woman who goes catching by night'. Malay sorcerers capture the souls of women whom they love in the folds of their turbans.

Souls of Gilyaks

According to Gilyak belief ordinary people have one soul, a rich man two, and a shaman may have up to four. At death the soul goes to the land of the dead where it assumes the form of a man, then it travels on from land to land, becoming smaller and smaller until it is as a speck of dust. Some souls are born again and return to Earth. The lesser soul lives for some time in the best loved dog of the deceased, which is especially cared for until the soul fragment returns to its master in the realm of the dead. The animal is then thrown on to the pyre.[7]

The Altaian *tula* soul belongs only to man. During a shamanic ceremony it is represented as a small white bullet continually in motion like quicksilver.[8] The soul is composed of various parts or exists in various stages. When a person is ill one soul (*suzy*) is absent, but another one (*tyn*) remains in the body so that the first may be recalled. (*Tyn* is derived from *tynip*, which means 'I breathe', or *tynit*, 'breath'. The *tyn* soul is vitality, and common to plants, animals and man.) If the first soul fails to return the *tyn* dies.

The *sūr* soul leaves the deceased and is banished from the dwelling for forty days after death; the *sūne* phase of the soul is peculiar to man and represents his intellectual powers. After death it assumes the deceased's likeness and wanders about in his house, sometimes calling out to relatives.

The Finnic tribes believe man is composed of body, shadow and soul. At death the soul passes into an infant of the same clan or into another clan if the first one is extinct. The person's shadow goes to the icy seas of the freezing underworld, situated beyond the mouth of the Ob, where he or she continues the same kind of life that was lived on Earth. Gradually the shadow gets smaller and smaller until it is no bigger than a black beetle. Some people believe that it turns into a beetle. Finally it disappears completely.

Anyone who came to know the words the shaman used to summon his spirit, that is, his soul, could easily cause his death. To kill him involved binding strips of rawhide on to a birch twig and turning it, saying: 'I squeeze the soul out of a [here follows a river name] shaman'.[9] The souls of outstanding dead shamans protect human beings, even as Christian saints protect the faithful.

The souls of the wicked, or of women who have died childless, have no sacrifices offered to them and their souls are one-eyed, malevolent spirits who remain in the same house and are particularly dangerous to children under 7 years old. Sometimes they assume the form of a one-eyed dog or cat and wander about at night. Not everyone can see them, but their presence may be recognized by their unpleasant smell. They are said to fear angry men, fire, metals and weapons.

Birarčens believe that the road to the underworld is long. The soul is watched by a raven who flies to the family of the deceased when the soul goes towards *buni*. Beyond this area is *èla gurum* from which the soul never returns – it is total death and the complete disappearance of the soul. The souls of newborn infants are not stabilized, so a number of precautions must be taken to keep the soul in the child's body.

To the Mongolian Daurs the term *sumus* ('soul') could refer to an immortal consciousness that after death would become an ancestor, or to a consciousness that was normally extinguished in sleep (but could leave the body in dreams) or to an entity that 'separated from the body at death, "changed appearance", and returned to the world in some other form'.[10] Various parts of the body had separate 'energies' or 'consciousness'.

Ainu underworld

According to the Ainus of Japan the soul of the deceased inhabits a body resembling that which it had in life and it will live in much the same way as during its lifetime. Souls may revisit the Earth as ghosts. All souls go finally to Pokna-Moshiri, the underworld which is divided into three parts: one leads to the world of the living, one to the world of deities, and the last to the 'wet underground world'. On the testimony of the fire goddess the soul is rewarded if it has led a good life and is punished if it has led an evil one. If the soul lies and denies having done evil, the individual is confronted with a picture representing his whole life which the fire goddess possesses, after which there is no point in denying one's wrongdoing.

It is said that men's souls perch on the branches of the World Tree – a myth common to Central Asia and Siberia. Evenki shamans never cut their hair because the souls of dead clan members live in it. Shamans can change themselves into birds and so recover the 'soul birds' on the World Tree. The archaic motif of a bird perched on a post often occurs in shamanic symbolism and also on the tombs of Yakut shamans. A bird on a post is depicted on a Lascaux relief in a scene which Horst Kirchmer suggests represents a shamanic trance, but not all scholars agree with this interpretation.[11]

Ancestor cults

Ancestors are highly regarded by all the clans. Among the Daurs the village graveyard is reserved for people destined to become ancestors, but not shamans or infants. Their bodies are exposed on the branches of trees so that their souls can return quickly to the world of the living. Some people could never become ancestors, including illegitimate children, unmarried girls, suicides, pregnant women and those who had died of infectious diseases. The latter were buried in unmarked graves some distance from the village.

According to the Buriats, the divine right (*utcha*) of shamans was formerly received from the celestial spirits, but now it comes from the ancestors which indicates decadence.

By drumming on his 'reanimated' drum fashioned partly from the skin of his chief helping animal, that is, his *alter ego*, the shaman 'changes into the mythical theriomorphic ancestor . . . the primordial animal that is the origin of his tribe'.[12] In this way he abolishes time when he returns temporarily to the mythical past.

Before the intrusion of Tsarism, Christianity and, finally, the Russian Revolution in 1917, the worship of ancestors spiritually united all the clan members, but by the end of the eighteenth century many of the old cults had been largely eradicated.

The Yukaghir clan system was mostly destroyed by the colonial system and by the disastrous smallpox epidemics of the late seventeenth and eighteenth centuries. Formerly, in memory of the shaman ancestor, the Yukaghirs made wooden figures of human beings and hung them on trees near mountain paths, estuaries or hunting areas. These figures were regarded as ancestors, and were consulted concerning important events; thus part of the old cult of Nature and her 'Masters' managed to survive.[13]

Many of the clans adopted some of the saints of the Russian Orthodox Church in addition to their own deities, especially as the saints were said to control specific animal species, as in the past the shamanic 'Masters' had done. Thus St Nicholas protects quadrupeds, St George birds, St Peter fish; all saints are appealed to in order to achieve success in hunting.

Formerly among the Kamens the headman of the community had a small, crudely carved, wooden figure depicting the ancestors. It was placed by the fire when the men went fishing and was thought to ensure a successful catch.

Not so long ago whalebone pillars could be seen representing the ancestors of the Chukchis. It was customary to hang amulets on them. They were addressed before hunting expeditions and offered the meat and fat from sacrifices.[14]

The Koryaks have specific detached mountains or cliffs which are regarded as ancestors of the clan who have been turned to stone. Most ancestors of the Mongols were soon forgotten, except for one, a shaman, who was in touch with a non-shaman clan ancestor who had become a spirit.[15]

Formerly the Daurs had a number of origin myths including the belief that they were descended from the union of a hunter and a vixen.

The vixen 'symbolized both the wild and "external", and femininity which was "internal" (human) but rejected'. Their greatest ancestor was envisaged as a pursued deer, probably because the Daurs lived in the region formerly set aside by the Manchus as their hunting grounds. 'Shamanic thought thus systematically negated the patriarchal version of smoothly succeeding ancestor generations. It encompassed all people and indeed all natural phenomena as ancestral.'[16] Another important ancestral spirit was Holieri who was only summoned when some disaster threatened.

Some of the ancestors of the Tungus-speaking groups could be dangerous to the living if their souls were unable to reach the next world; or they could become demons or ghosts.

Death and funeral rites

Shamans do not age as ordinary people do, for they have already undergone a kind of spiritual death when initiated. Henceforth, they are human vessels for spiritual powers by crossing the boundary between this world and the next, thereby taking up a new existence.

The dead bodies of shamans are sometimes placed in sacred groves which then become cultic areas, or on the branches or in the hollowed trunk of a birch tree, so that their souls may return quickly to this world. These trees are called the 'birches of the shamans', and if anyone should cut them down he would die immediately. Other methods included placing the corpse in a shallow depression in the steppe, or on a platform raised on four posts. Shamanesses were sometimes buried on mountain tops or in caves. After death both shamans and shamanesses become much more powerful.

When burial is in the trunk of a tree, the bark is replaced so that the tree continues to grow and the shaman's soul/spirit becomes the Master Spirit of the place. Those shamans of the Naun Daurs that were laid to rest on trees in remote places were soon forgotten, but many Siberian peoples remembered their shamans' graves for generations.

When Hailar Daur shamans are near death they examine their dreams to discover where they should be laid to rest. Later the bones are collected for a second burial, and placed in a white cloth sack with stones piled up around it, after which the shaman's pupil designates a nearby tree as a ritual tree. Every three years the next shaman of the lineage circumambulates the tree and venerates his ancestor. Buriats also venerate trees that have Master Spirits in them.

For winter burial a small hut is erected in the snow with a platform inside covered with white felt on which the corpse is laid. A post is erected nearby on which are placed the shaman's paraphernalia and ritual costume. The deceased is placed with his head facing west, and the platform is circumambulated in the direction of the sun. A naturally polished stone is placed under the head, the right cheek rests on the palm of the right hand and the body lies on its right side. The palm and fingers of the right hand cover the ear, mouth and right eye. The left palm rests on the left buttock. The legs are half bent and the eyes covered with a white ribbon because all the nine openings of the body must be closed at death. The deceased's position and the stone pillow 'probably indicate an ancient tradition dating back to Scythian times, when the body was folded up in the grave, with a stone under the head which was turned towards the west or north west'.[17] In the folklore of the Selkuts, mention is made of corpses being placed in cedar trees or larches, but never in birches.

Shirokogoroff describes the burial of a Tungus shaman of Transbaikalia.[18] The body was placed on a raised platform and most of his ritual objects were put either in the coffin or hung up on a nearby tree. A number of posts were erected and decorated with carved birds – birds that would help to carry away the shaman's soul. If anyone touches his belongings some mental illness will occur or even death.

The Chukchi dead travel difficult paths to reach the next world as well as passing through the country of dogs. If the deceased had ill-treated dogs in life he will be severely injured by them.[19] In Vedic Indian belief the two fierce dogs (Sārameyas) guard the way to the dead, as did the Greek Cerberus.

Nivkhi people believe that twins occur because their mother has had relations with a spirit in a dream. A mother of twins is treated differently from other women; she feels she belongs to another world. She is not cremated, which is the usual custom, but is laid in an open box covered with shavings. This is customary also for people who belong to the world of bears, for bears are the kin of twins. However, some of these women were able to adapt to their anomalous situation between the two worlds, and to obtain favours from the supernatural realm. In the Nivkhi language twins are called *n'a* ('animals'). The verb 'to die' for twins is *prijud* (for ordinary humans, *mud*). *Prijud* is used also for the death of a captive bear.[20] A number of stone and clay figures of bears were found in the Neolithic settlements of the Far East and on the Amur, and continued to be found into the nineteenth century.

Formerly, the Yukaghirs placed the dead on raised platforms, and distributed the flesh and bones among the relatives who dried their portion, placed it in a leather bag and wore it as an amulet called 'grandfathers'. Such amulets are considered to be effective for all magical purposes.

The Central and North Asian people have complex funerary customs much influenced by religious ideas from the South. Yakuts believe that good and bad souls ascend to the sky, where they assume bird form, but paradoxically they also believe that evil spirits, who are the souls of the dead, live underground.

Cremation is practised by the Buriats, Chukchis and Koryaks. The souls rise up to the sky in the smoke of the funerary fire, there to live a life resembling that which was formerly lived on Earth. Similarly, a person struck by lightning flies up to the sky, since fire of any kind purifies and transforms an individual into a spirit, and hence shamans are masters of fire and capable of touching hot coals without injury. In some respects being burned is a kind of initiation. Heroes who meet violent deaths also rise up to the sky, their death being regarded as an initiation.

People who die from disease (which is always caused by the hostile spirits of the dead) go to the underworld. Thus Altaians and Teleuts say that 'the dead are eaten by the dead'.

Horse sacrifice

A funerary banquet is held three, seven or forty days after death, when the deceased's favourite horse is sacrificed and eaten. Its head is placed on a stake stuck in the grave. Sometimes the soul of the deceased is reluctant to leave the world of the living, whereupon a shaman is summoned because only he possesses the power to lead it to the underworld.

The horse has long had a funerary aspect, being the mythical image of death; therefore it is incorporated into the archaic techniques of ecstasy. The sacrificed animals form large herds belonging to the dead. A dead layman's horse will either be slaughtered and burnt or allowed to go free. If it attempts to return it is driven away because, now being sacred, it is regarded as extremely dangerous.

Nivkhi, Tungus and Gilyak

Nivkhi people believe that the dead go to the village of the dead (*miy-vo*), then after a new death the soul goes down to another *miy-vo* where they either disappear or are reincarnated, but a woman's soul dies four times and is then resurrected.

Tungus believe, along with Muslims and Christians, that although everybody dies and everything disintegrates on Earth, individuals have a continued existence in other worlds. Muslims are provided with a number of beautiful girls in Paradise where they will experience an infinite orgasm,[21] and righteous Christians sit on the right hand of God. The Uda Tungus who live on the coast of the Sea of Okhotsk say that the dead go to a dark place to be united with their wives and children; those who die a sudden or violent death go to the Aurora Borealis. Depictions of boats on river banks in Siberia and Scandinavia are probably associated with an ancient concept of souls floating to their ancestors where the sun sets. Sometimes a moose or reindeer accompanies the boat of the dead. These ideas and myths arose 'during ancient times from concepts existing in a wide area of northern Europe and northern Asia. They were parts of an ancient world outlook.'[22]

According to Tungus belief the dead can harm the living or even carry them off to the world of the dead. A reindeer is killed at funerals to carry the deceased to the next world. When a corpse is in the house, dogs, cats and chickens are kept away lest a dog may carry a soul away before a shaman can accompany it and take all necessary precautions. If an animal jumps over a corpse and takes away the soul, or if it produces a draught that blows off the paper that covers the deceased's face, this will cause the dead to revive. The northern Tungus believe that a shaman's soul must be taken to the lower world by another, stronger shaman. If the soul is not conveyed to the world of the dead (*bunil*) it will never rest and will disturb the clan members.

Kumarčen and Khingan Tungus are usually buried in a hollow tree trunk rather than in coffins. The Transbaikalian Reindeer Tungus sacrifice a reindeer (or a horse if no reindeer is available) at the burial site; the inside of the coffin is smeared with blood. Then the animal is skinned and its hide, with its head facing northwest, is attached to a horizontal bar fixed to two trees and left hanging there. The flesh is cooked and shared out among the mourners except for a small piece which is left for the soul.

A dead Gilyak is tied to a sledge with his favourite dog placed next to him. For a few months the dog will receive and keep a portion of his master's soul. During this time the animal is well fed until the soul fragment returns to its master in the realm of the dead, when weapons, sledges, pans and the dog are thrown on to the funeral pyre.

During a shaman's funeral an arrow is drawn backwards to draw back the 'essence' to the family line, in the hope that one of the dead shaman's descendants will become a shaman, for an 'essence' not represented on Earth by a shaman is dangerous to its owners. The Yakut realm of the dead is situated in the north beyond the eighth heaven, a terrible region of eternal darkness and icy winds. There both girls and youths remain eternally virgin. Some Yakuts believe that the world of the dead is underground, and can be entered through an airhole left by the inhabitants of this subterranean region.[23]

Death caused by women

Death itself was blamed on women by the Samoyeds – a view based on the notion that female spirits caused death, for which women had to atone. (This shows an unconscious fear on the part of men of the power of independent women.) But both male and female shamans are prevented from attending funerals of ordinary people otherwise they would become defiled, although some clans see the shaman as a psychopomp – a most important task – so in this context he directs the funeral ceremonies and his spirit accompanies the soul of the deceased to the next world.

Methods of dealing with the dead

Among the peoples of Kamchatka and Chukotka there are various methods of dealing with the dead including cremation, burial, air burial or disposal at sea, but cremation and air burial are the most usual. In cases of voluntary death that sometimes occurs among the Chukchis and Koryak the person asks a friend or relative to strangle him or to kill him in some other way, after which all his belongings are burnt. In cases of natural death, complex rituals are performed including wiping the body with grass, thereby indicating that the deceased is being born in another realm. Reindeer were sacrificed by the Reindeer Chukchi and Koryak; among the Maritime clans, dogs were sacrificed to guard against hostile spirits. They were stabbed through the heart and grass collars put on them, and then they were hung up on poles erected around the village.

Certain privileged persons are cremated and rise up to the sky in the smoke to live in much the same way as they did on Earth. Shamans experience such deaths. Both the Chukchi and Koryak believe that fire transforms human beings into 'spirits' as well as being a form of initiation, for shamans are Masters of Fire.

Among the Inuits of the Bering Strait, certain male and female shamans own dead souls and supernatural beings called *tunghāt*. The more spirits a shaman owns the greater his powers. Dead people and animals answer his call as he journeys to the realm of the dead. He knows the rites and sacrifices required by the dead; he can change the weather and cure the sick, but if he ever uses his power for bad ends he may be killed.

When a shaman dies his costume has to be carefully looked after by a member of the next generation. This precaution was necessary because of the inherent magical power residing in its miniature weapons and ornaments – a power that extends into the future, for they are constantly interacting with the dangerous invisible powers which they were designed to destroy.

Some Mongolian Daurs believe that the female spirit Ome Niang-Niang possessed a special tree in the other world, where the souls of the dead remain in nests before turning round to enter the world of the living.

8

Images and Idols

Most images are of animals which for thousands of years were so important in the economic life of Siberian and other early peoples. Among the anthropomorphic images are the ancestor spirits and those of the cult of important female protective spirits called *emelgelči-ēren*. Vajnšteyn suggests that the name is derived from the Mongolian term *emeg* ('grandmother'). Sometimes they are represented by cloth dolls sewn on to felt. Such figures were inherited by Tuvan women and often buried with them.[1]

A large specific category of spirits, their receptacles and their images are called *ongons*; Tuvans called them *erens*, benevolent spirits that help shamans and other people. Vajnšteyn considers that *ongons* are pre-shamanic in Siberia, and later became an integral part of shamanist ideology and practice. They are made either by shamans or on their instructions, and may be fashioned from wood, metal or other material. Some images are in the form of masks.

The receptacles of the animal images are in the shape of some part of the animal's body. The main function of both human and animal types is to protect against disease-demons, so their receptacles are hung by the bedside, or placed at the entrance to a dwelling. Some images are so dangerous that they can be used only by shamans. Ribbons, leather fringes or beads decorate the receptacles to honour the spirits within. Sometimes they are 'fed' with a special nine-holed spoon.

The bear spirit was the most powerful of the Tuvan zoomorphic good spirits and is owned only by the most powerful shamans. Some receptacles were carved in bear shapes or fashioned from cloth; others consisted of dried bear paws. Such bear idols are known to most

Siberian clans, as are the snake figures. The snake image is made of red felt with the mouth open showing a felt tongue, eyes made of beads and with a copper horn attached to its head. These snakes are effective against rabies and cattle diseases. Sometimes a hare would be stuffed with grass and could be used both by shamans and laymen as an idol. The hare image was widespread in Tuva; it healed pain in leg joints, stomach ache and similar ailments. Some ethnographers see a connection between *ongons* and totems.

The Turks of the Western Siberian Baraba steppe are known as Baraba Tatars who were converted to Islam about the end of the eighteenth century. They had wooden figures that represented their spirits. These were kept far away from the settlement in a special hut in the care of a shaman. These huts were difficult to find, being off the beaten track. Sometimes the way was marked by rags hanging from the trees. Women were never allowed to enter the huts. On specific days, before the spring and autumn festivals, the shaman and some adults went to the idol hut to pray.

Kumandins have a few small drum idols consisting of a frame with two crossbars – one vertical, the other horizontal. The latter has a metal pendant attached and four wooden rings called 'earrings'.

Altaians make images, male and female, of their clan shamans' ancestors and hang them up in their dwellings. When N. Spafarij journeyed through Siberia in 1675, he saw temples containing silver, copper and wooden idols before which the Ostyaks prayed. Forty years later another traveller described temples erected by the Ob Ugrians which contained anthropomorphic wooden figures wrapped in rags.[2]

The Samoyed peoples kept their idols on wooden sledges. Shamans also used sacred sledges for storing their instruments. These sledges were different from ordinary ones which have two runners. These had three or four runners on each side. A chest covered with reindeer hide was placed on the sledge with the legs and frontlet still attached and with metal pendants, pieces of cloth and other sacrificial offerings. The front was regarded as the head of the spirit and was smeared with fat and blood; the runners represented legs. Two light-coloured reindeer bulls pulled the sledge which was led by a sexually immature boy or girl. No woman was allowed to touch it. The girths for the reindeer were made from white or brown bear- or sealskin, but no rope was used for the harness or for tying the sledge because rope was made by women who are considered impure. The Baraba Turks had idols in their drums and other images with pointed heads. The latter were also possessed by the Kumandins, the Mansis, Nenets, Khantys and Samoyeds. Some of the idols are now in the Tomsk Regional Museum.

Buriats have two kinds of *ongons*, some representing famous male or female shamans or princes who are masters of mountains, valleys, forests and so on to whom offerings are made. They protect the devout from all misfortune. The others represent spirits of individuals who have died untimely deaths, including suicides. These are weak spirits but dangerous to infants and cattle. Offerings to them take the form of a kind of ransom.[3]

The Dolgan peoples have man-made images of animals or of natural objects called *sajtāns*, as well as human figures called *bajanajs* which bring good luck to hunters.[4] When healing a sick person, the shaman tramples on a small stone. If the patient can find the stone, the illness will be transferred to it and remain there provided the patient keeps the *sajtān* which apparently functions as a kind of amulet. A special stone belonging to a deceased shaman is decked with gifts and placed on the skin of a polar fox with front teeth from a wild deer, necklaces and similar objects.

Ob Ugrians make wooden images of game animals and place them in sacred areas to ensure successful hunting and fishing. Some are drawn on living trees, as the Konda Ostyak do after catching a bear, elk or other animal. Its picture is painted on a pine tree in the village or along a path. The human horned figures on Finnish and Siberian rock paintings probably depict people shamanizing.

To the Daurs, the life of a single animal is important. To kill a doe which might embody a spirit could make women infertile. Therefore, hunters are careful to be respectful when a doe is killed. Some women kept images of deer and made offerings to them.

In 1988 Chinese film-makers made a film concerning the Manchu shamanism of the Jilin district. The ceremony started before daybreak. Offerings were made to the deities of agriculture, hunting, darkness and to the sky pole. Before each family's offering the clan chief and chief shaman opened the clan's ancestral box – a wooden chest containing genealogical records, images of the clan gods and other ritual items. The clan ancestors live in the box and the guardian spirits dwell above the ninth heaven. Four shamans took part wearing ceremonial skirts embroidered with cloud patterns and cone-shaped bells, the sound of which symbolized thunder. Through drumming and singing, they invoked the guardian god of farmers, Wuxinendure, requesting his protection and that he bring prosperity. A large black pig was sacrificed, cooked and placed on the altar. Deities were invoked to come down to the altar and share the meat. After dark most of the lights were turned off. The audience knelt while the shamans danced and sang, drumming ecstatically. Deities were evoked to give protection – primarily from the goddesses presiding over darkness and safety. On the following day the sky pole offering ritual took place. The pole was cut from a straight tree about three metres in height and representing the nine celestial levels. This sky pole is the way to the upper world and is erected in the middle of the courtyard. The top was smeared with a blood offering to the gods. Grain and pig intestines were attached to the pole as offerings to ravens and magpies, the sacred messengers of the gods. The shaman chanted and asked the gods for protection. Finally, offerings of food were hung on a willow tree, its many leaves being sacred to the fertility goddess Fuduo Mama. After the ceremony the pig bones were scattered on a mountain top or thrown into a river (mountains and rivers symbolize easy access to the other world).[5]

9

Were-Animals

It is necessary to know some of the religious ideas concerning animals behind the concept of were-animals. Humans, animals, birds and fishes all have immortal souls which, in successive lives can take on human, bird or animal forms. For this reason animals are not inferior to human beings, since a person may have a vestige of an animal soul because in a previous life it had belonged to an animal, and vice versa, for the soul never dies but only changes shape. However, this is not a systematized theory such as the concept of Buddhist *karma*, although both may have had common roots.

Although animals, birds, fishes, invertebrates and insects temporarily embody shamanic spirits, the creatures themselves are not worshipped. Animals too should engage in worshipping spirits as do humans. However, not every animal was regarded as embodying a spirit, but only if it behaved in a strange, unnatural way, or if it seemed to bring illness and bad luck to the individual seeing it. Yet some species appear to be vessels for spirits more than others. Thus among the Daurs the unpredictable and sly fox was greatly feared since it might embody devils, as well as the snake, porcupine and spider. Other spirit-animals are the tiger, bear, elk, maral deer, sable, eagle and some others. A shaman imitated these animals both in their movements and sounds. It is said that some animals, including the fox, snake, porcupine, pheasant and spider, could prolong their lives by ritual breathing techniques (*lien ch'i*). After 1,000 years they become black; after 10,000 years pure white, and extremely wise. Caroline Humphrey maintains that the were-animal cult was disseminated to the Manchus by Chinese Taoist and Buddhist monks, the Daurs and the Birarčen Tungus in the early part of the twentieth century.

Daurs kept small wooden shrines in their outhouses for the fox spirit, called Auli Barkan (mountain spirit). Auli Barkan was depicted as a fox with a human head, who protected against burglary but also caused insanity. It has been suggested that the 'ideas about fox spirits were a dense symbolic area on which the cult of were-animals was superimposed'.[1]

Shirokogoroff attended a number of were-animal performances among the Birarčen Tungus, in which the spirit flung itself about in the darkness causing the young men to fall over and cry out. The spirit drank vodka and yelled in Russian for more; various conjuring tricks occurred and also exorcisms. Daur, Mongol, Manchu, Chinese and other languages were used to address foreign spirits.[2]

The ancient were-animal cult was spread by wandering professionals, holy men or sorcerers who were widely travelled, and much more sophisticated than the ordinary villagers. During the nineteenth century Scandinavian shamans were said to be able to turn themselves into wolves and also to transform the dead into werewolves. The mere sight of a werewolf was enough to cause mental illness, whilst wolf packs were believed to be a number of corpses in the form of werewolves. Belief in metamorphosis into animal shape was common in Old Europe. According to the *Volsunga Saga* (5 and 8) the wearing of a wolfskin enabled the shape-change to occur. Such changes 'took place within the ecstatic states peculiar to the cult of Odin, to the belief in the Wild Hunt',[3] when ghostly riders ride the storms at the head of a spectral army.

In Old Prussia it was said that corpses, uttering terrible cries and surrounded by flames, would rise from graves in the form of wolves. In many cultures wolves are often the familiars of primitive gods of the dead. The Celtic wolf swallows the sun at night; the Aztec howling wolf is the god of the dance; the ancient Olmecs believed in werejaguars. To Christians the wolf represents the devil.

Notes

Two titles referred to frequently in the Notes below:

1 *Shamanism in Eurasia*, (eds) M. Hoppál with V. Diószegi
2 *Shamanism in Siberia*, (ed.) M. Hoppál

1 Male and Female Shamans

1 Shirokogoroff, *Psychomental Complex*, p. 118.
2 *The Rite Technique of the Siberian Shaman*.
3 'Finnish Rock Art, Animal Ceremonialism and Shamanic World View', p. 75, in *Shamanism in Eurasia*, and see also her *Studies on Shamanism*, p. 6.
4 R. Hamayon, 'Is There a Typically Female Exercise of Shamanism in Patrilinear Societies such as the Buryat?' p. 307 in *Shamanism in Eurasia*.
5 For further details see C.M. Taksami, 'The Story of a Nivkhi Shamaness as Told by Herself', pp. 309–313 in *Shamanism in Siberia*.
6 B.N. Basilov, 'Vestiges of Transvestism in Central Asian Shamanism', p. 288 in *Shamanism in Siberia*.
7 Eliade, *Shamanism*, p. 258
8 Basilov, ibid., p. 288f. See also, Eliade, *Shamanism*, p. 395.
9 Jochelson, *The Koryak*, Vol. 10, pt i, p. 52.
10 Bogoras, *The Chukchee*, p. 455.
11 W. Heissig, 'A Mongolian Source of the Lamaist Suppression of Shamanism', *Anthropos*, 48, pp. 1–29, 498–536.
12 Shirokogoroff, ibid., p. 364.
13 L. Delaby, 'Shamans and Mothers of Twins', p. 226 in *Shamanism in Eurasia*.
14 *Shamanism in Siberia*, p. 262.
15 Shirokogoroff, ibid. p. 371.
16 *The Non-Medical Use of Drugs, Interior Report of the Canadian Government's Commission of Inquiry* (1971), p. 151f.
17 Eliade, *Myths, Dreams and Mysteries*, pp. 59ff., and his *Shamanism*, pp. 96–99.
18 Kalweit, *Shamans*, p. 143.
19 U. Marazzi, 'Remarks on the Siberian Turkic Shamans' "Secret Language"', p. 281 in *Shamanism in Eurasia*.
20 E. Taube, 'South Siberian and Central Asian Hero Tales', p. 346 in *Shamanism in Eurasia*.

21 Eliade, *Shamanism*, p. 63.
22 Coxwell, *Siberian and Other Folk-Tales*, p. 283f.
23 Shirokogoroff, ibid., p. 118.
24 Alekseev, 'Helping Spirits of the Siberian Turks', p. 269 in *Shamanism in Eurasia*.
25 T. Domotor, 'The Problem of the Hungarian Female Taltos', p. 424 in *Shamanism in Eurasia*.
26 Cho Hung-youn, 'Problems in the Study of Korean Shamanism', p. 461 in *Shamanism in Eurasia*.
27 I. Ecsedy, 'The New Year's Tree and Other Traces of Ancient Shamanistic Cult in China', p. 109 in *Shamanism in Eurasia*.
28 Youngsuk, *Six Korean Women*, pp. 11ff.
29 Humphrey and Onon, *Shamans and Elders*, pp. 233 and 258, n. 90.
30 Czaplička, *Aboriginal Siberia*, p. 200, note citing Sieroszewski; see also Eliade, *The Forge and the Crucible*, ch. 8.
31 Popov, 'Consecration Ritual for a Blacksmith Novice among the Yakuts', *Journal of American Folklore*, 46, pp. 257–271.
32 Jochelson, *The Yakut*, pp. 172ff.
33 Popov, ibid., p. 260f.
34 Gaster, *Thespis, Ritual, Myth and Drama in the Ancient Near East*, p. 158. Stutley, *Dictionary of Hinduism*, p. 306.

2 Trance, Ecstasy and Possession

1 Johan Reinhard, 'Shamanism and Spirit Possession', in J. Hitchcock and R. Jones (eds) *Spirit Possession in the Nepal Himalayas*, p. 20.
2 Shirokogoroff, *Psychomental Complex*, p. 362.
3 Ibid., p. 364.
4 Kalweit, *Shamans, Healers and Medicine Men*, p. 72.
5 Mauss and Hubert, *Sacrifice. Its Nature and Function*, pp. 48, 129f. and n. 207; Westermarck, *Christianity and Morals*, p. 113. In 1215 the Fourth Lateran Council decreed that when the priest at the altar uttered the phrase 'Hoc est corpus meum' (this is my body) the bread and wine were changed into the body and blood of Christ. See Coulton, *Five Centuries of Religion*, I, p. 104; Jacob, *Six Thousand Years of Bread*, p. 162.
6 Frankfort, *Ancient Egyptian Religion*, p. 154. Stutley, *Dictionary of Hinduism*, under 'Hamsa', p. 108.
7 Curtin, *A Journey in Southern Siberia*, pp. 44–52.
8 Humphrey and Onon, *Shamans and Elders*, p. 30.
9 Eliade, *Shamanism*, p. 204 and n. 57.
10 E.W. Nelson, 'The Eskimo about Bering Strait', *18th Report of the American Bureau of Ethnology*, pp. 433ff. Washington.
11 Eliade, ibid., p. 506.
12 Simek, *Dictionary of Northern Mythology*, p. 35.

13 Ibid., p. 338.
14 Rohde, *Psyche*, I and II.
15 Kalweit, ibid., p. 57.
16 Ibid., p. 80.
17 *The Doors of Perception*, p. 155.
18 O'Brien, *Varieties of Mystic Experience*, p. 297f.
19 For some of Paul's archaic notions see Stutley, *Magical Elements of the Bible*, p. 131f. Alcohol and other drugs were used.
20 Eliade, *Patterns*, p. 108.
21 Batchelor, *The Ainu and their Folklore*, p. 308.

3 Shamans' Paraphernalia

1 See Eliade, *Shamanism*, p. 502, n. 23.
2 'History in Buryat Society', p. 208, in Voight, *Shamanism in Siberia*.
3 Stutley, *Dictionary of Hinduism*, under 'Aśvattha'.
4 Eliade, ibid., p. 170.
5 Donner, *La Sibérie. La vie en Sibérie, les temps anciens*, p. 230.
6 Shirokogoroff, *Psychomental Complex*, p. 297.
7 Czaplička, *Aboriginal Siberia*, p. 221.
8 V. Diószegi, 'Pre-Islamic Shamanism of the Baraba Turks', p. 111 and illustration, p. 112, in Voight, *Shamanism in Siberia*.
9 Ibid., p. 113f., citing Potapov.
10 Voight, *Shamanism in Siberia*, p. 258.
11 M. Jankovičs, 'Cosmic Models and Siberian Shaman Drums', p. 152, in *Shamanism in Eurasia*.
12 Ibid., p. 151, citing Potapov.
13 S.J. Vajnštejn, 'Shamans in Tuva at the Turn of the Twentieth Century,' p. 364, in *Shamanism in Eurasia*.
14 Ringgren, *Prophetical Conception of Holiness*, p. 23f.
15 A.V. Smoljak, 'Some Elements of Ritual Attire of Nanai Shamans', p. 245, in *Shamanism in Eurasia*.
16 A. Sárközi, 'A Mongolian Text of Exorcism', p. 329, in *Shamanism in Eurasia*.
17 Humphrey and Onon, *Shamans*, p. 224f.
18 Czaplička, ibid., p. 210.

4 Deities and Spirits

1 Czaplička, *Aboriginal Siberia*, p. 260.
2 Krader, 'Shamanism . . .', p. 186, in *Shamanism in Siberia*.
3 V. Diószegi, 'Pre-Islamic Shamanism of the Baraba Turks', p. 133, in *Shamanism in Siberia*.

4 Balzer (ed.), *Shamanic Worlds*, p. 100.
5 Krader, ibid., p. 196.
6 Czaplička, ibid., p. 258.
7 Ibid., p. 268.
8 Batchelor, *The Ainu and their Folklore*, pp. 248ff., 258.
9 Czaplička, ibid., p. 289.
10 Kalweit, *Shamans*, p. 199.
11 Ibid., p. 239.
12 Czaplička, ibid., p. 231.
13 Sieroszewski, 'Du Chamanisme d'après les croyances des Yakoutes', p. 336f, *Revue de l'histoire des religions, XLVI*, 1902.
14 Ibid., p. 303.
15 I.S. Gurvič, 'Culture Objects of Hunting among the Northern Yakuts', p. 484, in *Shamanism in Siberia*.
16 'Animistic Notions of the Enets and the Yenisei Nenets', p. 431, in *Shamanism in Siberia*.
17 Coxwell, *Siberian and Other Folk-Tales*, p. 231.
18 Z.P. Sokdova, 'The Representation of a Female Spirit from the Kazym River', p. 500, in *Shamanism in Siberia*.
19 Ju. B. Simčenko, 'Mother Cult Among the North Eurasian Peoples', p. 510f. citing Ansimov, in *Shamanism in Siberia*.
20 Ibid., p. 511.
21 Fitzhugh and Crowell, *Crossroads of Continents*, p. 255.
22 Shirokogoroff, *Psychomental Complex*, p. 125.
23 Ibid., p. 177.
24 J. Pentikäinen, 'The Sámi Shaman-Mediator Between Man and the Universe', p. 135, in *Shamanism in Eurasia*.
25 V.I. Vasiljev, 'Animistic Notions of the Enets and the Yenisei Nenets', pp. 435–437, in *Shamanism in Siberia*.
26 Humphrey and Onon, *Shamans and Elders*, p. 197.
27 Ibid., p. 213.
28 Ibid., pp. 286–293.
29 Ibid., p.217, n. 60.
30 Shirokogoroff, ibid., pp. 159f., 387.
31 Balzer (ed.) *Shamanic Worlds*, pp. 98, 93, 99f.
32 Siikala and Hoppál, *Studies on Shamanism*, p. 5.

5 The Shaman's Costume

1 Humphrey and Onon, *Shamans and Elders*, p. 208.
2 Czaplička, *Aboriginal Siberia*, p. 222.
3 Orgony, 'The Problem of Knots of Mongolian Shaman's Garment', *International Symposium of Mongolian Culture*, pp. 85–108.
4 Eliade, *Shamanism*, p. 158.

5   Shirokogoroff, *Psychomental Complex*, p. 296.
6   Eliade, ibid., p. 160.
7   S.J. Vajnštejn, 'Shamanism in Tuva . . .', p. 364, citing Okladnikov, in *Shamanism in Eurasia*.
8   'The Shaman as Social Representative in the World Beyond', p. 298f., in *Shamanism in Eurasia*.
9   Coxwell (ed.), *Siberian and Other Folk-Tales*, p. 422.
10 Vajnštejn, ibid., p. 365.
11 Siikala, 'Finnish Rock Art, Animal Ceremonialism and Shamanic World View', p. 76, citing Frolov in *Shamanism in Eurasia*.
12 Czaplička, *Aboriginal Siberia*, p. 215.
13 Ibid., pp. 211ff.
14 G.N. Gračeva, 'A Nganasan Shaman Costume', p. 318 in *Shamanism in Siberia*.
15 Ibid., p. 320.
16 B.D. Dolgikh, 'Nganasan Shaman Drums and Costume', p. 342, in *Shamanism in Siberia*.
17 Djakonova, 'The Vestments and Paraphernalia of a Tuva Shamaness', p. 338, in *Shamanism in Siberia*.
18 Shirokogoroff, ibid., p. 290.
19 Eliade, *Shamanism*, p. 177, citing Hoffman.
20 *La Sibérie. La vie en Sibérie les temps anciens*, p. 277.
21 Humphrey and Onon, ibid., pp. 206 and 253, n. 36, citing Haslund-Christensen. See also p. 207.
22 A.V. Smoljak, 'Some Elements of Ritual Attire of Nanai Shamans', p. 247, in *Shamanism in Eurasia*.
23 E.L. Lvova, 'On the Shamanism of the Chulym Turks', p. 241, in *Shamanism in Siberia*.
24 Humphrey and Onon, ibid., p. 209.

6 Divination and Healing

1   H.G. Creel, *The Birth of China, A Summary of the Formative Period of Chinese Civilization*, p. 21f.
2   E.L. Lvova, 'On the Shamanism of the Chulym Turks', p. 241, in *Shamanism in Siberia*.
3   Shirokogoroff, *Psychomental Complex*, p. 89.
4   Ibid., p. 352.
5   Lvova, 'On the Shamanism of the Chulym Turks', p. 241, in *Shamanism in Siberia*.
6   L.V. Khomič, 'A Classification of Nenets Shamans', p. 249, in *Shamanism in Siberia*.
7   Kalweit, *Shamans*, p. 45.
8   Humphrey and Onon, *Shamans and Elders*, pp. 227ff. and p. 257, n. 77.

9 Stutley, *Dictionary of Hinduism*, p. 290.
10 Kalweit, ibid., p.164.
11 Ohnuki-Tierney, 'The Shamanism of the Ainu of the North West Coast of Southern Sakhalin', pp. 15–29, and his *Illness and Healing Among the Sakhalin Ainu. A Symbolic Interpretation*.
12 Coxwell, *Siberian and Other Folk-Tales*, pp. 98–100.
13 Sargant, *The Mind Possessed*, p. 198.
14 Balzer, *Shamanic Worlds*, p. 154.
15 V.A. Tugolukov, 'Some Aspects of the Beliefs of the Tungus (Evenki and Evens')', p. 425, in *Shamanism in Siberia*.
16 S.J. Vajnštejn, 'Shamanism at Tuva at the Turn of the Twentieth Century', p. 361, in *Shamanism in Eurasia*.
17 Kalweit, ibid., p. 227.

7 Soul, Ancestor Cults and Death

1 A. Hultkrantz, 'Shamanism and Soul Ideology', p. 29, in *Shamanism in Eurasia*.
2 Czaplička, *Aboriginal Siberia*, p. 288.
3 Humphrey and Onon, *Shamans and Elders*, pp. 217ff.
4 L. Delaby, 'Shamans and Mothers of Twins', p. 218, citing Sternberg, in *Shamanism in Eurasia*.
5 L. Krader, 'Shamanism: Theory and History in Buryat Society', p. 193, in *Shamanism in Siberia*.
6 Shirokogoroff, *Psychomental Complex*, p. 134.
7 Czaplička, ibid., p. 273.
8 Ibid., p. 282.
9 V. Diószegi, 'Pre-Islamic Shamanism of the Baraba Turks', p. 112, in *Shamanism in Siberia*.
10 Humphrey and Onon, ibid., p. 213.
11 Eliade, *Shamanism*, p. 481, citing Kirchmer.
12 Eliade, *Shamanism*, p. 170.
13 I.S. Vdovin, 'Social Foundations of Ancestor Cult Among the Yukaghirs, Koryaks and Chukchis', p. 409, in *Shamanism in Siberia*.
14 Ibid., p. 416.
15 Humphrey and Onon, *Shamans and Elders*, p. 189.
16 Ibid., pp. 284 and 330.
17 M.B. Kenin-Lopsan, 'The Funeral Rites of Tuva Shamans', p. 297, citing Vajnštejn, in *Shamanism in Siberia*.
18 Shirokogoroff, *Psychomental Complex*, p. 382.
19 Czaplička, *Aboriginal Siberia*, p. 148.
20 L. Delaby, 'Shamans and Mothers of Twins', p. 226, n. 5, in *Shamanism in Eurasia*.
21 Hary, *Sexuality in Islam*, p. 80.

22 Martynov, *The Ancient Art of Northern Asia*, p. 37f.
23 Sieroszewski, *Du Chamanisme*, p. 206f.

8 Images and Idols

1 S.J. Vajnšteyn, 'The Ērens in Tuva Shamanism' , p. 457f., in *Shamanism in Siberia*, and see his 'Shamanism in Tuva at the Turn of the Twentieth Century',
   p. 355f., in *Shamanism in Eurasia*.
2 V. Diószegi, 'Pre-Islamic Shamanism of the Baraba Turks', p. 147, in *Shamanism in Siberia*.
3 L. Krader, 'Shamanism; Theory and History in Buryat Society', p. 203, in *Shamanism in Siberia*.
4 A. Popov, 'The Dolgan Sajtāns', p. 453, in *Shamanism in Siberia*.
5 For further details see Siikala and Hoppál, *Studies on Shamanism*, p. 194f.

9 Were-Animals

1 Humphrey and Onon, *Shamans and Elders*, pp. 101–106, 331f.
2 Shirokogoroff, *Psychomental Complex*, p. 235f.
3 Simek, *Northern Mythology*, p. 372.

Bibliography

Alekseenko, A.E. 'The Cult of the Bear among the Ket (Yenisei Ost-yaks)', in
V. Diószegi (ed.), *Popular Beliefs and Folklore in Siberia*, The Hague, 1968.

Anisimov, A.F. *The Social Organization of Events*, 1936.

Bäckman, L. and Hultkrantze, A. *Studies in Lapp Shamanism*, Stockholm, 1978.

Balzer, M. (ed.) *Shamanic Worlds*, New York.

Barthold, W. *Histoire des Turcs d'Asie Centrale*, Paris, 1945.

Basilov, B.N. 'Vestiges of Transvestism in Central Asian Shamanism', in
Shamanism in Siberia, pp. 281–289, Budapest, 1978.

Batchelor, J. *The Ainu and their Folklore*, 1901.

Bender, M. and Huana, S. *Daur Folktales*, Beijing, 1984.

Bethenfalvy, G. (ed.) *Altaic Religious Beliefs and Practices*, Budapest, 1992.

Blacker, C. *The Catalpa Bow. A Study of Shamanistic Practices in Japan*, London,
1975.

Bogoras, W.G. *The Chukchee*, American Museum of Natural History, Memoirs,
3, New York, 1904.

—— 'The Shamanistic Call and the Period of Initiation in Northern Asia and
Northern America', in *Proceedings of the 23rd International Congress of
Americanists* (1928), pp. 441–444, New York, 1930.

Bouteiller, M. *Chamanisme et guérison magique*, Paris, 1950.

Boyer, P. (ed.) *Cognitive Aspects of Ritual Symbolism*, Cambridge, 1993.

Browman, D.L. and Schwart, R.A. (eds) *Spirits, Shamans and Stars*, The Hague,
1979.

Cahill, S. and Halpern, J. *The Ceremonial Circle: Shamanic Practice, Ritual and
Renewal*, London, 1991.

Campbell, J. *The Masks of God: Primitive Mythology*, New York, 1972.

—— *The Way of the Animal Powers*, London, 1984.

Charles, L.H. 'Drama in Shaman Exorcism', *Journal of American Folklore*, 66
(260), pp. 95–122, April–June, Boston, 1953.

Christiansen, R.T. 'Ecstasy and Arctic Religion', *Studia septentrionalia*, 4,
pp. 19–92, Oslo, 1953.

Clark, C.A. *Religions of Old Korea*, Seoul, 1929.

Coomaraswamy, A.K. 'The Inverted Tree', *Quarterly Journal of the Mythic Society*, 29 (2), pp. 1–38, Bangalore, 1938.

Coulton, C.G. *Five Centuries of Religion*, 2 vols.

Coxwell, C.F. (ed.) *Siberian and Other Folk-Tales*, London, 1925.

Creel, H.G. *The Birth of China. A Summary of the Formative Period of Chinese Civilization*, 1936.

Curtin, J. *A Journey in Southern Siberia*, London, 1909.

Czaplička, M.A. *Aboriginal Siberia; A Study in Social Anthropology*, Oxford, 1914.

—— *My Siberian Year*, London, 1916.

de Groot, J. M. *The Religious System of China*, 6 vols, Leiden, 1892–1910.

DeKorne, J. *Psychedelic Shamanism*, Loompanics Unlimited, 1994.

Devereux, P. *The Long Trip. A Prehistory of Psychedelia*, Harmondsworth, 1997.

Diószegi, V. *Tracing Shamans in Siberia*, Netherlands, 1960; 1968.

—— (ed.) *Popular Beliefs and Folklore Tradition in Siberia*, Budapest, 1968.

—— 'Shamanism', *Encyclopaedia Britannica*, 16, pp. 638–641, London, 1974.

—— 'Tuva Shamanism', *Acta Ethnografica*, Vol. II, pp. 143–190, Budapest, 1962.

—— (ed.) with Hoppál, M. *Shamanism in Siberia*, Budapest, 1978.

Donner, K. *La Sibérie. La vie en Sibérie, les temps anciens*, Paris, 1946.

Dupre, W. *Religion in Primitive Cultures. A Study in Ethnophilosophy*, The Hague, 1975.

Eder, M. 'Schamanismus in Japan', *Paideuma*, 6 (7), pp. 367–380, May 1958.

Eisler, R. *Man into Wolf*, London, 1951.

Eliade, M. 'Le problème du chamanisme', *Revue de l'histoire des religions*, 121 (1), pp. 2f., 5–52, Paris, 1946.

—— *Patterns in Comparative Religion*, trans. Rosemary Sheed, London, 1958.

—— *Myths, Dreams and Mysteries*, trans. Philip Mairet, London, 1960.

—— *Images and Symbols*, London, 1961.

—— *The Forge and the Crucible*, London, 1962.

—— *Shamanism: Archaic Techniques of Ecstasy*, London, 1964.

Fairchild, W.P. 'Shamanism in Japan', *Folklore Studies*, 21, pp. 1–22, Peking, 1962.

Feng, H.Y. and Shryock, J.K. 'The Black Magic in China Known as Ku', *Journal of the American Oriental Society*, 55 (1), 1935.

Fitzhugh, W.W. and Crowell, A. *Crossroads of Continents*, Smithsonian Institute, USA, 1988.

Flaherty, G. *Shamanism and the Eighteenth Century*, Princeton, 1992.

Frankfort, H. *Ancient Egyptian Religion*, New York, 1948. Reprinted 1961.

Furst, P. (ed.) *Flesh of the Gods: The Ritual Use of Hallucinogens*, New York, 1972.

—— *Hallucinogens and Culture*, California, 1976.

Gaster, T. *Thespis. Ritual, Myth and Drama in the Ancient Near East*, New York, 1950; 1961.

Giedon, S. *The Eternal Present* (Mellon Lectures, 1957), London, 1962.

Gimlette, J.D. *Malay Poisons and Charm Cures*, 1915; reprinted Oxford, 1991.

Gjessing, G. 'Circumpolar Stone Age', *Acta artica*, 2 (2), Copenhagen, 1944.

Goloubew, V. 'Les tambours magiques en Mongolie', *Bulletin de l'École Française d'Extrême-Orient*, 23, pp. 407ff., 1923.

Goodman, F.D. *Where the Spirits Ride the Wind: Trance Journeys and Other Ecstatic Experiences*, Indianapolis, 1990.

Granet, M. 'Remarques sur le taoïsme ancien', *Asia Major*, 2, pp. 145–151, Leipzig, 1925.

Hallowell, A.I. 'Bear Ceremonalism in the Northern Hemisphere', *American Anthropologist* (Menasha), 28, pp. 1–175, 1926.

Hancar, Franz, 'The Eurasian Animal Style and the Altai Complex', *Artibus Asiae*, 15, pp. 171–194, 1952.

Harner, M.J. *Hallucinogens and Shamanism*, Oxford, 1973.

—— *The Way of the Shaman*, San Francisco, 1990.

Harva, U. *Finno-Ugric and Siberian Mythology*, 1927.

—— *The Shaman Costume and Its Significance*, Annales universitatis fennicae aboensis (Turku) series B, 1 (2), 1922.

Hary, A.B. *Sexuality in Islam*, London, 1985.

Hatto, A.T. *Shamanism and Epic Poetry in Northern Asia*, London, 1970.

Heissig, W. 'A Mongolian Source of the Lamaist Suppression of Shamanism', *Anthropos*, 48, pp. 1–29, 498–536, 1953.

—— *The Religions of Mongolia*, translated from German by G. Samuel, London, 1980.

Hermanns, M. *Mythen und Mysterien, Magie und Religion der Tibeter*, Cologne, 1956.

Holm, N.G. (ed.) *Religious Ecstasy*, Stockholm, 1982.

Holmberg, U. and Harva, U. *The Shaman Costume and its Significance*, Turku, 1922.

Hopkins, L.C. 'The Shaman or Chinese Wu: His inspired Dancing and Versatile Character', *JRAS*, 1–2, pp. 3–16, 1945.

Hoppál, M. (ed.) *Shamanism in Eurasia*, Göttingen, 1984.

—— 'Shamanism: An Archaic and/or Recent System of Beliefs', *Ural-Altic Yearbook*, 57, pp. 121–140, 1985.

—— with Diószegi, V. (eds) *Shamanism in Siberia*, Budapest, 1978.

—— with Howard, K.D. (eds) *Shamans and Cultures*, Istor Books, 5, Budapest, 1993.

—— with Paricsy, P. (eds) *Shamanism and Performing Arts*, Ethnographic Institute Hungarina Academy of Sciences, Budapest, 1993.

—— with von Sadovszky, O. (eds) *Shamanism Past and Present*, Istor Books, 1–2, Budapest, 1989.

Hori, I. 'Penetration of Shamanic Elements into the History of Japanese Folk Religion', in E. Haberland, *Festschrift for Adolf Jenson*.

Hultkranz, A. 'A Definition of Shamanism', *Temenos*, 9, pp. 25–37, Helsinki, 1973.

Humphrey, C. 'Shamans and the Trance', *Theoria to Theory*, 5 (4), 1971, 6 (1), 1972.

Humphrey, C. and Onon, U. *Shamans and Elders*, Oxford, 1996.

Huxley, A. *The Doors of Perception*, London, 1954.

Jacob, H.E. *Six Thousand Years of Bread. Its Holy and Unholy History*, New York, 1944.

Jochelson, W. *The Koryak*, American Museum of Natural History, Memoir 10, New York, 1905–1908.

—— *The Yakut*, Anthropological Papers, 33, Part 2, 1933.

Joralemon, D. and Douglas, S. *Sorcery and Shamanism*, Utah, 1993.

Kalweit, H., *Shamans, Healers and Medicine Men*, trans. M.J. Kohn, London, 1992.

Kamata, H. 'Daughters of the Gods: Shaman Priestesses in Japan and Okinawa', in J. Pittau (ed.), *Folk Cultures of Japan and East Asia*, Monumenta Nipponica Monographs, 25, Tokyo, 1966.

Kaplan, R.W. 'The Sacred Mushrooms in Scandinavia', *Man*, 10, 1975.

Karlgren, B. 'Contributions to the Shamanism of the Tibetan–Chinese Borderland', *Anthropos*, 54, p. 802, 1959.

Katz, R. 'The Painful Ecstasy of Healing', *Psychology Today*, December, pp. 81–86, 1976.

Kim Taegon, *A Study of Shaminism in Korea*, Korean Shamanism, Series 4 (8), Seoul.

Kitagawa, J. 'Ainu Bear Festival (Iyomante)', *History of Religions*, 2 (1), 1961.

Krader, L. 'A nativistic movement in Western Siberia', in *American Anthropologist*, vol. 58, 1956.

Kroef, J.M. van der, 'Transvestitism and the Religious Hermaphrodite in Indonesia', *Journal of East Asiatic Studies*, 3, pp. 257–265, Manilla, 1959.

La Barre, W. *The Ghost Dance*, New York, 1972.

—— 'Hallucinogens and the Shamanic Origins of Religion', in P. Furst (ed.), *Flesh of the Gods*, New York, 1972.

Larsen, S. *The Shaman's Doorway*, New York, 1976.

Laufer, B. 'Origin of the Word Shaman', *American Anthropologist* (Menasha), 19, pp. 361–371, 1917.

—— 'Burkhan', *JAOS*, 36, pp. 390–395, 1917.

Lessing, F.D. 'Calling the Soul, a Lamaist Ritual', in *Semitic and Oriental Studies*, pp. 263–284, Los Angeles, 1951.

Lewis, I.M. *Ecstatic Religion*, London, 1971.

—— *Religion in Context. Cults and Charisma*, Cambridge, 1994.

Lindgren, E.J. 'The Reindeer Tungus of Manchuria', *JRAS*, 22, pp. 221–231, April 1935.

Liu, Mau-tsai 'Der Niang-Niang Kult in der Mandschurei', *Oriens Extremus*, 1972.

Lommel, A. *Shamanism: The Beginning of Art*, New York, 1967.

Lönnqvist, B. 'Problems Concerning the Siberian Shaman Costume', *Ethnologia Fennica*, 1–2, Helsinki.

Lopatin, I.A. 'A Shamanistic Performance to Regain the Favor of the Spirit', *Anthropos*, 35–36, pp. 352–355, 1940.

Lot-Falck, E. 'L'Animation du tambour', *Journal Asiatique*, 259, pp. 213–239, Paris, 1961.

—— *Les rites de chasse chez les peuples sibériens*, Paris, 1953.

Martynov, A. *The Ancient Art of Northern Asia*, Illinois, 1991.

Mauss, M. and Hubert, H. *Sacrifice: Its Nature and Function*, trans. W.D. Halls, Chicago, 1964.

Michael, H.N. *Studies in Siberian Shamanism*, Toronto, 1963; reprinted 1972.

Mikhailovski, V.M. 'Shamanism in Siberia and European Russia' (Part 2 of *Shamanstvo*), *Journal of the Royal Anthropological Institute*, 24, pp. 62–100, 126–158, 1894, translated from Russian by Oliver Wardrop.

Mironov, N.D. and Shirokogoroff, S.M. 'Śramaṇa-shaman: Etymology of the word "shaman"', *JRAS* (Shanghai), 50, pp. 105–130, 1924.

Munro, N.G. *Ainu Creed and Cult*, London, 1962.

Nakamura, H. *Ways of Thinking of Eastern Peoples*, London, 1964, 1997.

Narcotics, Bulletin on, 21 (3), July–September, United Nations, New York, 1969.

Nebesky-Wojkowitz, R. de 'Tibetan Drum Divination, "Ngamo"', *Ethnos*, 17, pp. 149–157, 1952.

Neher, A. 'A Physiological Explanation of Unusual Behaviour in Ceremonies involving Drums', *Human Biology*, 34 (2), pp. 151ff., 1962.

Non-Medical Use of Drugs Interior Report of the Canadian Government's Commission of Inquiry, 1971.

O'Brien, E. *Varieties of Mystic Experience*, New York, 1964.

Ohnuki-Tierney, E. 'The Shamanism of the Ainu of the NW Coast of Southern Sakhalin', *Ethnology*, 12, pp. 15–29, 1973.

—— *Illness and Healing Among the Sakhalin Ainu, A Symbolic Interpretation*, Cambridge, 1981.

Orgony, P. 'The Problem of Knots of Mongolian Shaman's Garment', *International Symposium of Mongolian Culture*, edited by Z. Jun-ji, 1993.

Popov, A.A. 'Consecration Ritual for a Blacksmith Novice among the Yakuts', *Journal of American Folklore*, 46 (18), pp. 257–271, July 1933.

Prince, R. (ed.) *Trance and Possession States*, Montreal, 1968.

Rahmann, R. 'Shamanistic and Related Phenomena in Northern and Middle India', *Anthropos*, 54, pp. 681–760, 1959.

Rasmussen, K. *Intellectual Culture of the Iglulik Eskimos*, Copenhagen, 1930.

—— *The People of the Polar North. A Record*, compiled and edited by G. Herring, 1908.

Rätsch, C. *The Dictionary of Sacred and Magical Plants*, Bridport, 1992.

Reinhard, J. 'Shamanism and Spirit Possession', in J. Hitchcock and R. Jones (eds), *Spirit Possession in the Nepal Himalayas*, Warminster, 1975.

Rinchen, Y. 'Noms des chamanes et des chamanesses en mongol', *L'Ethnographie*, pp. 74f., 148–153, 1977.

Ringgren, H. *Prophetical Conception of Holiness*, Leipzig, 1948.

Rock, J.F. 'Contributions to the Shamanism of the Tibetan-Chinese Border-land', *Anthropos*, 54, pp. 796–818, 1959.

Rohde, E.S. *Psyche*, I and II, Heidelberg, 1893.

Rouget, G. *La musique et la transe*, Gallimard, Paris, 1980.

Roux, J-P. 'Eléments chamaniques dans les textes pre-mongols', *Anthropos*, 53, 1–2, pp. 440–456, 1958.

Ruben, W. 'Schamanismus im alten Indien', *Acta orientalia*, 17, pp. 164–205, 1939.

Rubin, V. (ed.) *Cannabis and Culture*, The Hague, 1975.

Rudenko, S.I. *Frozen Tombs of Siberia*, published in Moscow 1953; in England 1970.

Salmony, A. *Antler and Tongue: An Essay on Ancient Chinese Symbolism and Its Implications*, Ascona, 1954.

Sargant, W. *The Mind Possessed*, London, 1973.

Schmidt, W. *Ursprung der Gottesidee; eine historisch Kritische und positive Studie*, vol. 3, pp. 333–339, Munster, 1912–1955 (12 vols in all).

Schultes, R.E. and Hofmann, A. *Plants of the Gods*, 1979.

Shi Kun 'Flying Drums, Dancing Shamans: Shamanic Practices among the Manchu of Northern China', *Shaman's Drum*, 25, pp. 22–29.

Shirokogoroff, S.M. 'General Theory of Shamanism among the Tungus', *JRAS* (Shanghai), 54, pp. 246–249, 1923.

—— *The Psychomental Complex of the Tungus*, London, 1935.

Shternberg, L.I. 'Shamanism and Religious Election', in S.P. Dunn (ed.), *Introduction to Soviet Ethnology*, Vol. 1, Berkeley, 1974.

Sieroszewski, W. 'Du Chamanisme d'après les croyances des Yakoutes', *Revue de l'histoire des religions*, 56, pp. 204–233, 299–338, 1902.

Siikala, A-L. *The Rite Technique of the Siberian Shaman*, FF Communications 220, Helsinki, 1978.

—— 'Finnish Rock Art', in *Studies on Shamanism*, Helsinki, 1992.

Siikala, A-L. and Hoppál, M. *Studies on Shamanism*, Budapest, 1992.

Simek, R. *Dictionary of Northern Mythology*, translated by Angela Hall, Cambridge, 1993.

Skeat, W.W. *Malay Magic*, London, 1900.

Strömback, D. 'The Realm of the Dead on the Lappish Magic Drums', *Artica*, Uppsala, 1956.

Stutley, M. *An Introduction to the Magical Elements of the Bible*, Zennor, 1991.

Stutley, M. and Stutley, J. *A Dictionary of Hinduism*, London, 1977.

Summers, M. *The Werewolf*, London, 1933.

Taksami, A.M. 'Survivals of Early Forms of Religion in Siberia', in M. Hoppál (ed.), *Shamanism in Eurasia*, Göttingen, 1984.

Tart, C.T. (ed.) *Altered States of Consciousness*, New York, 1972.

Tcheng-tsu Shang 'Der Schamanismus in China', Dissertation, Hamburg, 1934.

Vdovin, I.S. 'The Study of Shamanism among the Peoples of Siberia and the North', *Ninth International Congress of Anthropological and Ethnographical Sciences*, Chicago, 1973.

Voight, V. 'Shamanism in Siberia', *Acta Ethnographica*, 26, pp. 385–395, 1977.

Waley, A. *The Nine Songs: A Study of Shamanism in Ancient China*, London, 1955.

—— *Ballads and Stories of Tun-huang*, London, 1960.

Wasson, R.G. and Kramrisch, S. *Persephone's Quest: Etheogens and the Origins of Religion*, London, 1986.

Westermarck, E. *Christianity and Morals*, London, 1939.

Winstedt, R. *Shaman, Saiva and Sufi: A Study of the Evolution of Malay Magic*, London, 1925.

Wittkower, E.D. 'Trance and Possession States', *International Journal of Social Psychiatry*, 16 (2), pp. 153–160, 1970.

Yetts, P. 'Disposal of Buddhist Dead in China', *JRAS*, pp. 699–725, July 1911.

Yasser, J. 'Musical Moments in the Shamanistic Rites of the Siberian Pagan Tribes', *Pro-Musica Quarterly*, March–June, pp. 4–15, London, 1926.

Youngsuk, K-H. *Six Korean Women. The Socialization of Shamans*, St Paul, New York, 1979.

Index